D0240375

LIFEBOAT VC

LIFEBOAT VC

The Story of Coxswain
Dick Evans BEM
and His Many Rescues

IAN SKIDMORE

DAVID & CHARLES
NEWTON ABBOT LONDON NORTH POMFRET (VT)

British Library Cataloguing in Publication Data

Skidmore, Ian
Lifeboat VC
1 Evans, Dick 2. Lifeboat service – Wales – Moelfre, Gwynedd – Biography
I. Title
361.5'8 VK1430.E/
ISBN 0-7153-7691-8

First published 1979
Second impression 1979

Printed in Great Britain
by Redwood Burn Limited
Trowbridge & Esher
for David & Charles (Publishers) Limited
Brunel House Newton Abbot Devon

Published in the United States of America
by David & Charles Inc
North Pomfret Vermont 05053 USA

CONTENTS

This book is dedicated with the deepest respect and transcendent admiration to DICK EVANS, *to the crews, living and dead, of the Moelfre lifeboat and to all lifeboatmen everywhere.*

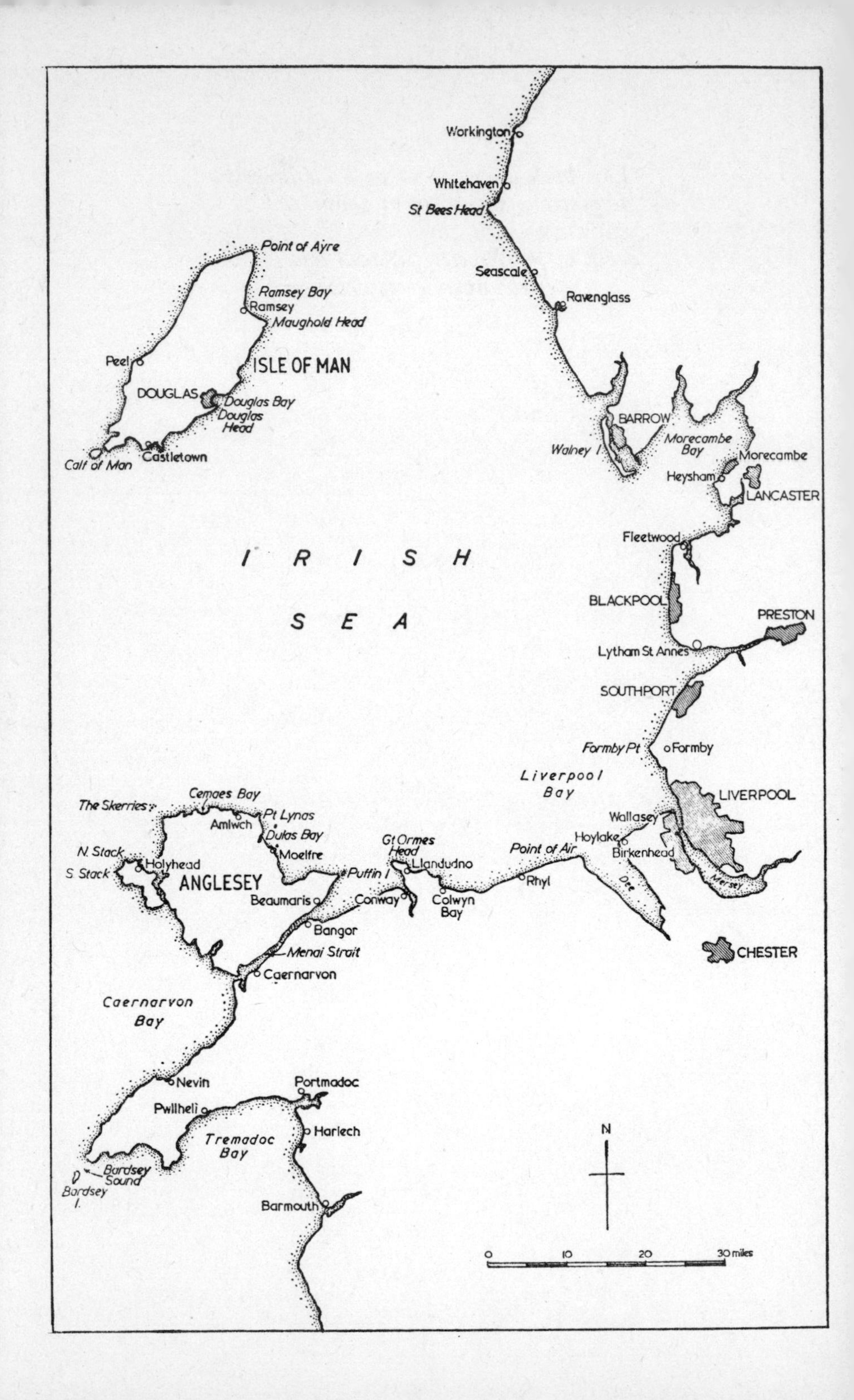

Workington
Whitehaven
St Bees Head
Seascale
Ravenglass
Point of Ayre
Ramsey Bay
Ramsey
Maughold Head
Peel
ISLE OF MAN
DOUGLAS
Douglas Bay
Douglas Head
Calf of Man
Castletown
BARROW
Walney I.
Morecambe Bay
Morecambe
Heysham
LANCASTER
Fleetwood
I R I S H
S E A
BLACKPOOL
PRESTON
Lytham St Annes
SOUTHPORT
Formby Pt
Formby
Liverpool Bay
LIVERPOOL
The Skerries
Cemaes Bay
Amlwch
Pt Lynas
Dulas Bay
Moelfre
N. Stack
S. Stack
Holyhead
ANGLESEY
Puffin I
Beaumaris
Gt Ormes Head
Llandudno
Conway
Colwyn Bay
Point of Air
Rhyl
Wallasey
Hoylake
Birkenhead
Dee
Mersey
Bangor
Menai Strait
Caernarvon
CHESTER
Caernarvon Bay
Nevin
Portmadoc
Pwllheli
Tremadoc Bay
Harlech
Bardsey Sound
Bardsey I.
Barmouth
N
0
10
20
30 miles

I

THE GREAT STORM

It drives on with a mercy which does not
quail in the presence of death.
It drives on as a truth, a symbol, a
testimony that man has been created in
the image of God and valour and virtue
have not perished in the British race.

Sir Winston Churchill

In the Anglesey fishing village of Moelfre, where houses gather like a frown on a headland overlooking Liverpool Bay, the people are used to wild weather.

Over a hundred years ago, on 25 October 1859, when the fiercest gales in living memory had lashed the coasts of Britain, Moelfre had been hit by the worst of them. The first shipping to be caught had been the sailing ships of the Channel Fleet at exercise off the Eddystone. Gusts of over 100mph sent them sliding into the troughs of mountainous waves. That was at 3pm. At 8pm the storm, which by this time had torn away coastal embankments and chewed up railway lines in Devon and Cornwall, reached Anglesey.

Outside Holyhead harbour the iron paddlesteamer, *Great Eastern*, was soon in danger; inside, ships sank at their moorings or were smashed into a flotsam of broken spars. The next day an even wilder storm hit Liverpool Bay. Ships dragged their anchors and were hurled on to rocks; at Flint a factory was levelled when its chimney was blown down.

Liverpool Observatory recorded the highest-ever wind force —28lb to the square foot—and the sea level rose 4ft. The Meteorological Office recorded the gale as 'a complete horizontal hurricane'; but, at Moelfre, Charles Dickens was one of many reporters who described the events in more harrowing terms. For it was there that the worst disaster of those terrible two days occurred. In a force 12 gale, when the winds gusted at over 100mph, the auxiliary steam clipper, *Royal Charter*, in passage from the Australian goldfields, was drawn on to the rocks outside the village, within sight of her home port of Liverpool. The vessel had brought her passengers, mostly miners returning home with their gold, halfway round the world when she sank with the loss of 450 lives.

During the storm 133 ships were sunk and 90 damaged; 800 lives were lost—twice as many as had been lost at sea during the whole of the previous year. The storm has always been known to seamen as the *Royal Charter* Gale; every year, a service of remembrance is held in Llanallgo Church where those bodies which were recovered from the wreck are buried.

Among the congregation on 26 October 1959 were the men of the Moelfre lifeboat, led by their fifty-four-year-old coxswain, Richard M. Evans. As they left the church after the service and walked down the path between the graves, Dick turned to his wife, Nansi, a farmer's daughter who was always upset by this commemoration of tragedy at sea. 'Don't worry,' he comforted her. 'We'll never have to launch the lifeboat in seas like that.'

He was to be proved wrong within twenty-four hours for the wind had been blowing hard all night and by morning it was a full gale.

Donald Murley Francis, an engineering fitter who was second coxswain of the lifeboat, had been worried since he left his cottage to go to work on 27 October. A seaman all his life he reacted to weather like a scientific instrument. A tiny, darkly Celtic man, with eyebrows like angle-irons, he moved like a ship's cat. At 10.30, an 80mph gale was blowing and he came to a decision; leaving the factory, he turned his steps towards the village. He knew he would be needed.

Burly Evan Owen, greying and merry-eyed, was at work at the lifeboat station from early in the morning. He had been the station mechanic since 1946, and, apart from Dick Evans, was the only member of the crew employed full-time by the Royal National Lifeboat Institution. He was usually to be found in the minute engine-room of the lifeboat, polishing, inspecting, testing his engines. A wartime RAF mechanic, he knew instinctively that lives depended on his skill.

Hugh Owen, the bowman, had been with Dick Evans since they both pulled an oar on the sailing lifeboat. Although never a deep-sea man, he was an expert in a small boat. A stone mason by trade, he had been obliged by lack of work to take a job as road foreman with Anglesey council. Almost at the moment Murley Francis walked out of the factory gates that morning, Hugh Owen said goodbye to his council road gang and walked the two miles to the village. At his side was another council employee, Hugh Jones, who had never been a member of the crew.

Dick Evans, Murley Francis, Evan Owen and Hugh Owen made a formidable team bonded together beyond their individual strengths by reciprocal respect. Dick Evans would often say that if Murley, Evan and Hugh were with him he would take the lifeboat to hell and back. He was shortly to get the chance.

Dick Evans is the archetypal seafaring man. With a healthy complexion, clear blue eyes, broad shoulders, a 44in chest and hands like crane grabs, he stands 5ft 9in tall and has the quick rolling walk taught by a lifetime on wet decks. That morning he was helping Nansi lay the places for lunch in the kitchen of their semi-detached home on the outskirts of Moelfre. From time to time he glanced out of the window as the gale worsened. He knew that the lifeboat was certain to be called out and the thought worried him.

To a coxswain his boat is a personal possession. Over the years he learns how she will react to every turn of weather or malice of tide. He needs to know whether she will take a beam sea and how she would run before a gale. The best cox is the one who eliminates as many risks as he can and then faces bravely those which remain. But, only the day before, the 42ft, Watson-class *Watkin Williams*—the boat Dick had commanded for three years—had gone for servicing to the boatyard at Beaumaris, several miles round the coast. His only experience at sea with the reserve lifeboat, *Edmund and Mary Robinson*, had been in bringing her round from Pwllheli. He had taken four of the crew by taxi to Pwllheli, where the *Edmund and Mary Robinson* was moored, and all the way he had been nagged by what Commander Dutton, the RNLI Chief Inspector, had told him on the telephone. 'She's given a great deal of trouble during her service. Do your best with her and telephone me the moment you reach Beaumaris, whatever time of day or night.'

They had cast off from Pwllheli at 7am into Bardsey Sound. Almost at once the 6-knot tide turned against them and, despite two 45hp diesels, the boat barely managed to creep through the neck of water between Bardsey Island and the mainland. At Caernarfon, Dick decided to wait for the tide to drop before tackling the 'Swellies', a stretch of rock-strewn channel in the Menai Strait which extends for a mile between the Britannia Tubular Bridge in the west and the Menai Suspension Bridge in the east. It was 8pm before they moored the lifeboat on a buoy at Beaumaris.

The passage had taken thirteen hours but Dick still knew very little about the new boat except that in her handling she was totally different from the *Watkin Williams*. Twenty-three years older the *Edmund and Mary Robinson* had none of the modern navigational aids of his usual boat. Dick would be uneasy until he had the feel of her.

At 11.50 that morning of 27 October the telephone rang and Dick went into the hall to answer it. It was Captain Owen Roberts, a retired ship's master who was volunteer duty coastguard at Moelfre watch tower. 'There's a ship dragging her cable in the bay,' he said. 'It doesn't look good. She was sheltering from last night's south-wester but the wind is veering rapidly to the north and she's been caught. She's being blown on to the rocks. All the other ships that were in the bay last night have managed to get out to sea, but she's trapped. She's the *Hindlea* out of Cardiff, 506-tonner. In ballast from Manchester to Newport.'

Essential information exchanged, Dick put the phone down and went back into the kitchen. 'Got a service,' Dick told Nansi briefly. 'Have to go.'

Nansi is a handsome, happy woman with a captivating laugh, but there was no trace of it as she watched Dick walk away. The moment he closed the front door Dick knew that he faced the most difficult service of his career. In forty years at sea he had never known such a wind. It was a full gale from the north; 90mph, he judged, and still increasing. Blowing from the sea on to the shore, it gave the worst possible conditions for a launch, Dick thought, as he struggled leaning on the wind, to the boat-house. Slates torn from the roofs smashed at his feet; they had the cutting edge of an axe and often he had to dodge as one hurtled towards him. From village barns, balls of hay bowled down the street like tumble-weed; other skeins festooned the telegraph wires. Tentacles of seaweed torn from the rocks whirled over his head like airborne octopuses to land in the gutterings of houses.

From Dick's house the road drops gently as it curves round the bay; then it climbs the headland to run through the upper village. There a path leaves it and follows the line of the cliff top to the lifeboat station with its slipway to the sea.

When he left the shelter of the cottages on the eastern face of the headland the full force of the gale struck him and for the only time that day he was grateful it was blowing on-shore—from any other quarter it would have swept him from the cliff top on to the rocks 30ft below.

The sea was frightening. As far as the horizon it had become a moving mountain range of grey water. Waves bigger than he had ever seen, some higher than houses, scrambled white crested over each other's backs. He began the slow struggle along the cliff top to the lifeboat station, dragging himself hand over hand along the iron railing at the edge.

Captain Roberts was waiting for him, sheltering under a wall. He looked anxious.

'I hate having to send you out in this, Dick,' he said. 'But that ship will soon be driven on to the rocks and once she gets into the breakers you won't be able to get near her.'

Murley, Evan, Hugh Owen and Hugh Jones were already in the boat-house. As Dick pushed open the door, the roar of the wind was muffled by the sound of the lifeboat engines. There was little hope of rounding up a full crew; telephone wires were down all over the island, and maroons would be useless in this weather. His glance fell on Hugh Jones. He had never been to sea in a lifeboat, even on exercise, but Dick needed every hand he could muster.

'Will you volunteer?'

The reply was equally brief. 'Of course,' Hugh Jones said and reached out for a life-jacket.

Each man knew that to take a small lifeboat totally unfamiliar to them into such seas was dangerous in the extreme. A man caught in a wild storm at sea has two choices: he can be brave or he can be cowardly. A special sort of courage is needed, however, to leave a safe home, walk down a village street and step deliberately into a situation of grave danger. These five men had taken that step and they would not turn back.

Dick clambered up the ladder on to the deck of the lifeboat and lashed himself to the wheel, which was corded to give a surer grip.

'Let's go, boys,' he said. One by one the crew followed him aboard.

'Check each other's life-jackets,' he ordered. 'Make sure they are properly fastened.'

He watched them tying the holding tapes; the jackets would be of little use in the seas they were going to meet, but there was reassurance in the familiar routine. By now the gale was gusting to 104mph. An identical wind had driven the *Royal Charter* on to the rocks a century earlier. That wreck, below low water mark, was half a mile along the cliffs from the lifeboat station where Dick and his skeleton crew of four were about to put to sea.

Even in calm weather the ride down the slipway is heart-stopping. As the *Edmund and Mary Robinson* raced through the open doors the waves reached up to drag at her. She hit the water like a bomb, submerging her bow completely in the boiling sea. Instantly she righted herself and the crew scrambled about the deck, hauling up the radio mast.

The propellers bit into the water and the first cloud of spray, like shattered glass, was flung into Dick's face. He stood behind the inadequate protection of a low screen, bracing himself against the padded back-rest. As always in the first moment of a service, Dick prayed. Unless some power outside himself came to his aid, he and his crew were dead men. He had learned his seamanship from his grandfather, who had passed on the accumulated sealore of centuries, but not even he had told him how to cope with 40ft waves coming from every point of the compass. When he prayed, Dick felt strength flowing into his arms and he was to need it. The words of the prayer, like all the commands in the boat, were Welsh: *O Arglwydd Arwain Fi* . . . (Please God Guide Me).

Dick was not afraid of the lifeboat sinking, but when they left the shelter of land he watched the slow run of each wave growing bigger with every yard and towering above sullen deeps and he knew it was in real danger of capsizing. Modern lifeboats, it is claimed, will right themselves in seven seconds in any seas. Older boats, like the *Robinson*, are always in danger of capsizing. Beam seas slammed into the lifeboat's wooden ribs, half turning her over. The radio mast touched the water and the men under the canopy were thrown into a tangled heap of sea boots and oilskins.

One moment the lifeboat would be climbing almost vertically up a 30ft wave, briefly seesawing on the crest, and the next she plunged into a trough. Each mountainous wave rose to an upward curl that threatened to engulf them. The impact of a second wave could send the *Robinson* somersaulting. Dick ordered acceleration to full revs on each crest, hoping the momentum would carry the boat to the peak of the next. Up and down she went, like a switchback car. Each time the prow of the boat buried itself in a trough, the men feared they would never resurface, but somehow they always did. Her deck canting, water thundering on the iron canopy, the lifeboat ploughed on through the maelstrom. To Dick, lashed to the wheel, drenched to the skin and blinded by foam and scud whenever he raised his head above the windscreen, it seemed they would never reach the coaster.

The *Hindlea* was less than half a mile from the slipway but it was an hour before they saw her. Dulas Bay, a sand-and-shell-bottom anchorage, was safe in southerly gales, but the gale blowing from the north was forcing the coaster inexorably into the breakers. She was lying to her starboard anchor in 8 fathoms of water. Every attempt by the crew to get to the fo'c's'le to put out the forward anchor had been defeated by the heavy seas crashing over her decks. She was heeling sharply and her engines were straining the single-anchor cable to breaking point. As the lifeboat crew watched, the

100-fathom cable whipped clear of the rough seas and the coaster was propelled towards the jagged plateau of rocks. The lifeboatmen could do nothing until the *Hindlea* skipper, Roland Chipchase, a fifty-four-year-old Tynesider, ordered his crew of seven to abandon ship.

As they waited they played a violent game of pat-a-cake to bring life back into their frozen hands and Dick beat his palms against the corded wheel. With the tide setting to the south-south-east, it was a constant battle to keep the *Robinson* head to sea on the starboard beam of the coaster. At last, at 1.55pm, an hour and a half after the lifeboat had taken up her station, the order was given to abandon ship. By now she was inside the 5-fathom line within 200 yards of the rocks and huge seas were breaking over her decks. The crew edged their way along the port side of the poop deck, clear of the round of the coaster's stern.

Edging towards the *Hindlea*, Dick wished he could have put out a drogue; but there was too little sea-room astern. The drogue, a conical sea anchor on a 10-fathom cable, would have kept the *Robinson* head on to the breaking sea and taken some of the crippling strain from his arms as he fought with the wheel. His strength alone could hold them stable. He ordered maximum revolutions, for as soon as speed was reduced his boat was thrown back by the seas. Now he put her on the lee of the *Hindlea*, but the coaster was tossing so wildly that he found himself coming up on the weather side.

Suddenly, through the white cloud of spray, he saw a glint of metal and felt his heart somersault. The violent pitching of the coaster had lifted her stern clear of the sea and her propellers, 9ft from tip to tip, were cutting through the air only 10ft above the bow of the lifeboat. In that same moment a snarling escarpment of water hit the *Robinson*. Dick felt the turbulence of air from the propellers as the blade came within inches of his head. Then the *Robinson* was sent rolling on her beam ends, her mast disappearing under the water. Using every scrap of skill to bring the lifeboat under control, Dick fought with the wheel, an insistent voice bursting in his head: 'It's the end. She's capsizing.'

Incredibly the *Robinson* did not capsize. Engines screaming at full revs, fighting the pull of the sea, she answered to the helm. A second wave, smaller than the first, righted her and, her deck shuddering, she slammed against the steel plates of the *Hindlea*. One of the crew, bolder than the rest, jumped from her poop and landed with a crash of sea boots on the lifeboat. Ignoring the dangerous pitching of the deck which every moment threatened to catapult him into the sea, Hugh Owen dashed out from the canopy and dragged the seaman to safety.

As the sea carried the *Robinson* clear of the ship, Dick realized that the only way they could hope to rescue the crew was to repeat the dangerous manoeuvre. He would have to bring the boat back under the propellers and hold her by the ship's side long enough to give the men on board an opportunity to drop into the lifeboat.

The second approach almost ended in disaster. On her run in, the *Robinson* was caught by the gale and suspended in mid-air, level with the deck of the *Hindlea*. Dick could have reached out and touched the white, frightened faces of her crew as the *Robinson* raced past, before crashing into a trough. The next attempt would have to be made when the *Hindlea* once more heeled to port and the lifeboat could take advantage of the meagre shelter of her poop.

Ten times the *Robinson* went alongside. On three occasions, she came away empty handed, but on the other approaches men jumped to the lifeboat and were grabbed to safety from the wave-washed deck.

There was only one member of the crew left aboard the *Hindlea*. Twelve men were now on the lifeboat. Dick had stretched his luck to breaking point and the *Robinson* had taken heavy punishment. Sturdy though she was, there was a limit to the pounding she could take from the seas and the constant crashing against the steel hull of the *Hindlea*. Even if she held together, could she make the passage back to Moelfre? Would it not be wiser to avoid the risk of further damage to the lifeboat? But as he weighed the alternatives Dick knew there was only one answer. He could not sail away leaving the last man to his fate. He turned the wheel and made his final run in.

The eighth man was over the coaster's side, hanging desperately from the rail. As Dick watched, a figure in oil-skins emerged from the lifeboat's canopy. He could not see who it was, but he took his hand from the wheel to give a brief encouraging wave. They came round the *Hindlea*'s stern, passing under the madly spinning propellers. In the engine room, Evan Owen responded instantly to every command for 'revving', and with surges of power, now forward, now aft, the *Robinson* edged towards the poop. Behind him Dick could hear the dry whine of the prop-shaft.

There was an explosion of light and spray. Over his head Dick saw the steel wall of the *Hindlea* rearing away. The propellers seemed to be cackling with malicious laughter as Dick felt the lifeboat lifting under his feet and the wind under the keel. The sudden shift of the *Hindlea* had again exposed the rescuers to the worst of the weather and a steam-rollering wave hurled them out of the water. They were flying.

Dick braced himself for the crash that would come when the *Robinson* dropped back in the sea; his hands were ready on the wheel to turn the boat in an instant out beyond the reach of those propellers. But the impact was so violent that the wheel was wrenched from his grasp. He was flung, winded, against his metal back-rest. Choking for breath he managed to grab the wheel and haul himself upright. He was uninjured but, as he looked around, he was stunned by what he saw. The lifeboat had landed on the deck of the *Hindlea.*

There was no way out now. The next wave would tip them, like rubbish from a bin, over the side bow-first into the sea. Dick threw a despairing glance towards the canopy and the men with whose lives he had gambled and lost. He had a split-second picture of the families of his crew—grouped wives, mothers and children on the headland at Moelfre, straining for a sight of the returning lifeboat. He had known them all their lives. He thought of his own wife, who could never join the group on the headland, for she had always to stay within earshot of the phone. She would be sitting with his two younger sons, listening fearfully to news bulletins on the radio, waiting, dreading the sound of the telephone ringing. A great wave of love for his family flooded over him. In that moment he loved them more than he had ever loved them in his life. He did not want to die, lashed to a lifeboat wheel, his body ripped by rocks. What right had he to take his crew to their deaths in an attempt to save the lives of eight men he did not even know?

The deck shifted violently under his feet and for a moment he thought that the *Hindlea* was breaking up under him. It was the second wave. He felt the *Robinson* once again lifting and surging forward, while behind and below him he heard the rush of water. Miraculously the wave, which by any reckoning should have swamped them, had lifted the boat clear of the deck. As she was swept back over the side, he saw Hugh Owen and Hugh Jones struggling to hold the last survivor. They had plucked him to safety as the wave carried them past.

It was 2.11pm by the time all the men were off the *Hindlea*; there was only one injury, a broken ankle. There were no casualties among the lifeboat crew and despite the hammering she had received, the *Robinson* had sustained no irreparable damage.

Steering her away from the *Hindlea,* Dick realized their mission still had a perilous course to run. The boat was on a lee-shore within 100 yards of some of the most dangerous rocks on that coast—a toy in a breaking sea. The survivors were in a bad way and his own men were beginning to show the effects of their ordeal. Dick's waist was raw and bleeding where the ropes tying him to the wheel had chafed at the skin. He had been soaked by the first burst of spray when the boat was launched and the salt had caked on the fresh cuts so that every movement he made was a burning agony. His sea boots, brimming with water, encased his lower legs and feet which felt as if they were fashioned from clumsily modelled clay, and there was no response from his toes when he braced himself against sudden movement. The muscles in his legs were taut like knotted wet bed sheets. His face was white and his eyelids gummed into narrow slits by the sea salt which crumbled like an Arctic landscape at every movement of his head. His hands were frozen to the wheel and he had long since lost any feeling in them. His numbed fingers could never unfasten the rope which secured him. If the boat capsized, he would be dragged over the rocks that came ever nearer.

The added weight of the eight survivors made the lifeboat sluggish. She rode low in the water and the breakers round the *Hindlea* threatened to engulf them. There was little room to manoeuvre between the coaster, which was already beginning to break up, and the rocks on the shoreline. More than ever Dick needed the aid of a drogue, but to order one of the crew to set it would be too dangerous. The passage to the comparative safety of the open sea was long and tricky; he had to nurse the boat every yard of the way.

He had to get the *Robinson* back to Moelfre. There would be a fire in the chapel vestry where the good women of the village would be waiting with hot food and drink and dry clothing. The prospect encouraged him; he screwed up his face to clear the salt from his eyes and set course for home.

Each breaker had to be met head on; the quiet water beyond provided the opportunity to go abeam until a second wave reared its head of tangled spume and sea-wrack. Deserted by gulls, the waters on the far side of the breakers resembled the crusted surface of an empty planet. Each swell encircled a shallow crater of water and beyond there were wave crests like crumbling cliffs.

The logical way back was on the weather side of Moelfre island, a dangerously rocky outcrop beyond the headland which protected the village beaches. The inner channel, while giving some shelter from the hurricane, was treacherous and in that sea there was little chance of navigating it safely. They would have to take the outer course where they would be at the mercy of the worst of the weather.

Under the stormy sky the *Robinson* rode the seas in scything sweeps that reminded Dick of the fairground boats of his childhood, spinning out above the heads of the crowd. But there were no ribbons of upturned faces to comfort him on this mad ride, no reassuring blare of the hurdy-gurdy, only the wild music of the gale and the seas as the little lifeboat pitched and rolled. A change in the sea sound told him they were near the island. The waves could be heard pounding against rocks but, strain though he might, he could not see them. He ploughed on, with the knowledge that close at hand rocks like plough blades waited, menacing.

In the event a single wave that must have been over 30ft high lifted the *Robinson* on to its cowled crest and carried her, planing helplessly half out of the water, past the length of the island before dropping her in quieter water beyond the tide-rip.

Dick has no memory of the ensuing minutes. Somehow he brought the lifeboat on to the moorings; the crew and passengers were taken ashore and he found himself blinking in the bright light of the chapel vestry. His next conscious recollection is of walking across the fields behind the chapel to the lifeboat station. Blood from cuts on his face, where he had rubbed it to clear his vision, mixed with salt and ran into his mouth to lie, bitter-sweet, on his tongue. He stomped, rather than walked, like a toy bear in oilskins, his legs rigid, his arms stiff at his sides.

Dick recalls:

> I sat on the slipway utterly exhausted. Suddenly I realized that tears were streaming down my face. They were tears of joy. My crew and I had saved eight men from a certain death and I felt very happy about it. By now everyone knew about the rescue; the ships were all talking about it. My own son, David, was chief officer on a tanker, the *Pass of Balmaha*, hove to in the Bristol Channel. The captain had told him when he went up to relieve him that a lifeboat was out somewhere off the British coast on a lee-shore in a 104mph hurricane. My son, who had been out in the boat with me on several occasions, said to the captain, 'Surely there's no lifeboat out on a lee-shore in this wind expecting to save lives?'
>
> 'That's what all the ships are saying,' the captain said.
>
> My son was pacing backwards and forwards in the wheel-house. He heard one ship say, 'I'm sorry for those lifeboatmen, they'll never get out of that.' Then he heard another ship. 'My God, that lifeboat's got the crew off. It was the Moelfre lifeboat.'
>
> David leaped down to the captain's cabin three steps at a time. He told him, 'Captain, Captain, it's my old man that's out in that lifeboat.'

Back in Moelfre, Dick reported to RNLI headquarters. 'The boat's badly damaged, but her engines are all right and she's still seaworthy.'

'Belay that,' he was told. 'Don't you dare take that boat

out again until she's had a thorough inspection by your district inspector.'

Twenty-five minutes later, however, the Moelfre lifeboat was launched again.

'Breaking the rules,' Dick says, recalling what happened. 'I was continually breaking the rules, but what else could we do? The *Essari*, formerly the *Pass of Lennie*, sister ship to my son's, was lying 3 miles off the slipway. Her engine room was flooded and she was dragging her anchor. Besides I wasn't worried. The sea was totally different by then. We were able to get a line aboard her and only had to wait 20 yards off her stern in case we were needed. Anyway, we knew that the Beaumaris lifeboat had been launched to relieve us. A terrible passage those lads had, too, coming from the Sound in Beaumaris into a northerly hurricane. But they arrived, bless them, and we were able to return to station.'

But not, even then, to rest.

'I sent the crew home,' Dick goes on, 'and then the mechanic Evan Owen and I stayed up all night in the boat-house trying to patch the boat up. Six o'clock the next morning I received a call to go out again to relieve the Beaumaris boat. I fired the maroon and to my amazement those same four lads came pounding down the path again, Y'know lifeboatmen do have tremendous guts. You've got to be with them to realize the kind of men they are.... Myself, I look on the RNLI as a truly Christian organization. Surely anything that saves lives in the terrible world we are living in today must be the finest kind of Christianity?'

It was 5pm on 28 October when, at last, the lifeboat returned to the slipway.

'I live about half a mile from the station but I was so tired I couldn't walk,' Dick recalls. 'I had to stop every few yards to rest. I got into the house at last and I slumped into the old armchair. I'm not a good sleeper usually but I fell asleep, or unconscious, I don't know. Anyway, my wife told me afterwards that I had her very frightened because every so often I was leaping out of the chair. Probably I was dreaming. . . .'

For this truly remarkable feat of seamanship and his outstanding courage in one of the most daring sea rescues of the century Cox'n Evans was awarded the RNLI gold medal—the first to be presented for ten years—known to the world's seamen as 'The Lifeboat VC'.

Motor-mechanic Evan Owen was awarded the silver medal; Donald Murley Francis, Hugh Owen and Hugh Jones each received bronze medals for their part in the rescue. The medals were presented by HRH Princess Marina, Duchess of Kent, then president of the RNLI.

Two years later, in 1961, at a ceremony at Buckingham Palace, Her Majesty the Queen presented the five lifeboatmen with the Silver Medal for Gallantry at Sea.

One other tribute remained to be paid. In 1964 the *Watkin Williams* again went in for her five-yearly refit. When her replacement chugged into Moelfre Bay the cliffs were lined with the seamen and their families who make up most of the population of the village. As she approached the slipway, elderly sea captains raised their trilbies and fishermen their stocking caps, while a ragged cheer broke out.

After serving at every lifeboat station from Land's End to the north of Scotland, the *Edmund and Mary Robinson* had come back to the lee-shore of her legend.

2

APPRENTICESHIP TO THE SEA

Dick Evans was born in 1905 in a terraced cottage on the cliffs. From his bedroom window he could look down over Moelfre Bay to the broad sweep of Red Wharf Bay and beyond that to Snowdon. As a boy, it was always to the sea he looked first in the morning. On rough nights the house was blanketed in spray from the reaching sea at the foot of the cliff. When he and his sister Kitty awoke, they would sit at the bedroom window watching the rollers in the bay below. They played a game of ships, riding the five oceans of the world on the bridge of an imaginary liner.

It was inevitable that Dick should become a seafarer. To go to sea was the dream of every boy in the village; to have had any other ambition would have been unthinkable. His father, William, was a sea captain, commodore of his line, and a member of the lifeboat crew of which Dick's uncle was coxswain. One grandfather had been second cox, the other a member of the crew. Dick was to carry on a family tradition. When, in time, he became coxswain, his three sons served under him in the crew. There were practical reasons for family crews. When Dick was a boy, there was no telephone in the village, no lights in the streets. If the coxswain and the second cox each had a couple of sons at home, a crew was immediately on hand to launch the lifeboat when a ship was in distress.

Until the influx of 'strangers' from the outside world in the 1950s, Moelfre was more of a family than a village.

Everyone was in some degree related to each other. Young men were discouraged from marrying outside the tightly knit sea-going families in the village. A boy who married into the farming communities lost status in the eyes of his neighbours.

Dick's father was away at sea for seven months of the year; every summer his mother would leave the children in the care of their grandparents and join her husband on his coaster. Dick loved those summers. Richard Matthews, his grandfather, never learned to read or write, but he was a man of many talents. He was the local butcher, a fine seaman, and the houses he built with his own hands stand firm and square in the village to this day.

Occasionally the sea took lives from the village, but each year it yielded a rich harvest of herring. In the days when a seaman's pay was little more than 30 shillings a week, the extra money earned from herring trawling was vital to the survival of his family. Every September when the shoals arrived off the island and the coasters were paid off, the seamen returned to the village and the herring harvest began. Nets and gear were made ready, and a fleet of up to thirty 20ft fishing boats—*Stag*, *Betty Ann*, *Sovereign*, *Seagull*, *Shamrock*—each with four men pulling at heavy oars, set off from the beach at night in search of the herring. Next morning the village children crowded on the headland to watch the boats returning, loaded to the gunwales with silver fish that glinted like coin in the early light. When they were sighted, another 'fleet' of ponies and traps came rattling down the village street, bringing dealers from all over Anglesey. Down the beach they swayed and rolled, so that carts and fishing boats met in the shallows and deals were struck as waves broke round the ponies' legs.

The herring were sold by the 'hundred'—perversely, 123 fish—counted out in threes by the fishermen in each boat in turn. This stately litany by a male voice sea choir rose over the crash of waves against the shingle. When the count of forty was reached, three extra fish were passed over to make sure that no buyer was given short measure; then the count would begin again at forty-one.

In the early part of the century there were always sailing ships in the bay; next to the herring fleet, the coalers provided the best free show for the children. These, too, had names more romantic than their calling: *Village Belle*, *Iris* and *John Nelson*; but the one that conjured up the great romance for Dick was *Mary Goldsworthy*. It was the ambition of every boy in the village to serve aboard that ship; on the evening she put in, the children were allowed to stay up late to watch her discharge her cargo. It was a valuable lesson in handling a vessel. A kedge-anchor was brought ashore and buried in the beach. Then, with two stern ropes put out to steady her, the 100-ton sailing ship was brought near enough to the shingle beach for the coal carts to drive into the shallows for the unloading.

The skipper, Captain William Roberts, was a great favourite; when his ship was safely anchored, droves of children would swim up alongside, each one to be rewarded on deck with a piece of iron-hard ship's biscuit.

Every hundredweight of coal was hand-winched from the hold by two seamen into the carts. The fully loaded cart would be drawn by three horses over the shingle, the third horse being taken out to pull the next cart into the shallows at the ship's side. It usually took three days to discharge a cargo of coal. When *Mary Goldsworthy* was empty and she was riding high in the water, it was time for the last and most interesting act to begin.

Familiar with every manoeuvre, the village children watched as a boat put off from the *Mary* with the kedge-anchor on a 100ft cable which was dropped on the firm bottom. Laboriously the ship was pulled round on the axis of the anchor until she was facing seaward. With a hollow rattling of blocks, Captain Roberts, quick as a fox, swarmed up the rigging, the sails were set and, to the waves and shouts of the children, the *Mary* got under way for the return passage to Point of Air colliery.

'I'd sooner be captain of the *Mary Goldsworthy*,' Dick solemnly told his sister, 'than a doctor or a surgeon or even a Member of Parliament.'

It was some years before Dick appreciated the hazardous economics of coaling. With coal at 10 shillings a ton, wages for a crew of three to pay and the risk of an east wind leaving a ship weather-bound in the Menai Strait for up to a fortnight, a skipper can have had little reward after meeting such expenses out of his share of the profits. Competition for cargo was keen. Down the coast at Red Wharf Bay sailing ships were glad of a load of turnips to take up to Liverpool.

In the days before World War I, when Dick's father was earning £7 a week as a captain, every fresh gift from the sea was rapturously received. Herring, mackerel, even seaweed gathered from the rocks in small boats and used to manure the potato crops, were the subject of thanksgiving prayers. The chapel was the centre of activity and villagers attended three times every Sunday. If for any reason they missed chapel, the children were afraid something terrible would happen to them. At 9.30 on Sunday morning Dick was sent to put on his best navy serge suit and the family set off for chapel. At 11.30 they returned; Dick changed out of his best clothes and sat down to dinner. At 1.45 the best clothes went on again for Sunday School, came off again at 3.30, went on again for the evening service at 6.10, came off for the last time at 7.30pm.

'I'm wearing them out quicker taking them off and on,' Dick complained, 'than I would if I kept them on all the time.'

Tuesday was 'Band of Hope' night. After the hymns and

the music lesson there was always a story of the sea or questions about knots and how to rig a sailing ship. Even at home the sea was used as a bribe. When Dick showed any reluctance to eat his bread-and-treacle breakfast his mother could easily overcome it by drawing the outline of a ship on his bread with the trickle of treacle as it came out of the tin.

It was the trips in grandfather Matthews' 20ft sailing boat, *Seagull*, which Dick remembers best. At 4am, if the tides were right, Dick was out of bed the second he heard his grandfather whispering through the bedroom door. A moment later he was dressed; five minutes for bread and treacle and a mug of hot, sweet 'seafarer's tea', then the old man and the boy would creep out of the house. Outside they could hear the crash of waves on the beach and the rattle of the shingle as the water ran back over the pebbles. To the small boy in the jersey and to his grandfather too, it seemed the most exciting sound in the world as, hand in hand, they hurried down the village street to the shore where the *Seagull* was beached above the high-water mark.

The old man made his own nets, even the difficult conical trawls few of the other fishermen would attempt. A number of meshes must be lost in every row as the trawl narrows to the cod end in which the fish are trapped. He also made the *Seagull*'s sail and the mast, whittling and sanding the unshapen wood as he sat by the hour at his cottage door.

Once the boat was safely launched, the lessons began. 'You've got to nurse a boat, boy,' explained the old man, a massive silhouette straddling the thwarts, denser than the dark around him. 'When a breaking sea is coming at you, bring the boat head on into her. Then, when the wave passes, you can put her back on course.'

When they reached the fishing ground the trawl was put out, well clear of the boat so that the mesh did not tangle in the tiller. For two hours they trawled companionably, listening to the wet laughter of the sea as it nuzzled into the

Seagull's side, while the trawl net dragged fathoms below gathering fish.

Sunlight spread across the horizon as, hand over hand, gnarled, calloused fingers rubbing like rope-ends against the boy's smooth fist, the two drew up the trawl. One final pull and the boat was dancing with life and light as the fish tumbled out of the nets at their feet. If there were oysters the old man seized them with delight. With a hand as horny as the shell it held, he would prise one open with his knife and, tipping his head back, pour the contents down his throat. Dick watched with astonishment the first time he saw him do this. The old man grinned. 'Eating the sea, boy,' he explained and, reaching into the bottom of the boat amongst the dazzling array of fish, found another oyster, opened it and passed it to his grandson.

As the smooth, salty oyster flesh filled the boy's mouth a wave of nausea rose in his throat. To vomit would be to disgrace himself; his grandfather would think he was seasick. He would be the laughing stock of the family and might never be allowed on the *Seagull* again. Somehow he had managed to calm his turbulent stomach and, by the time they reached Moelfre, his balance was quite restored. But he had learned his lesson. From that day all the oysters they found he very generously left for his grandfather.

When his grandfather went off to sell the fish, Dick, at nine an impressive figure in oilskins and miniature sea boots, was allowed to play in the boat on his own and take his special mates for a sail in the bay.

School interrupted this halcyon existence. Dick could splice a rope and rope a sail, but he was not interested in the chronicle of dead kings, the unpredictable behaviour of adjectives and adverbs, or the work-stained march of a column of figures down the page of an exercise book.

The location of the hilltop village school did little to help his concentration. From the classroom windows the pupils had a panoramic view of Moelfre Bay where up to sixty sailing ships could be riding at anchor or in passage to Ireland or Liverpool from the North Wales ports. Moelfre Bay is a good holding anchorage, providing shelter for whole fleets of ships from unfavourable north-westerly winds. The boys in Dick's class might be unsure which jaw-cracking city was the capital of Sweden, but they could identify every ship they saw by the set of its sails and the rig of a mast.

The headmaster, Mr Edwards, had the firm hand necessary to control his spirited pupils. Since Edwards was Church of Wales, the boys were not required to salute the ministers from the chapels; but, if they saw the vicar or the headmaster, even a quarter of a mile away, they had to spring to attention and salute. The habit died hard. When, years later, Dick—an ex-coaster skipper by that time with his fiancée on his arm—saw his old headmaster in Bangor, he automatically saluted. Beatings at school were frequent. Each child had a double peg for his cap and coat; to put the cap on the lower peg reserved for the coat would result in a sound thrashing.

Mr Edwards' tongue was feared as much as his hand. Once, during a geography lesson, Dick watched through the window a sailing ship tacking in the bay. The subject of the lesson was Nova Scotia, but Dick was with the sailing ship. He knew exactly what each member of the crew would be doing. The voice of the headmaster startled him.

'Richard, point out Nova Scotia!'

When Dick pointed uncertainly to the heart of Africa on the blackboard map, Edwards was less than pleased. Glancing at the sailing boat he said drily: 'As well you were only lowering the sail. You would scarcely be welcome as a navigator.'

Despite Dick's maritime preoccupations his talent for leadership made him an ideal class monitor. Whenever the headmaster felt the need for a moment of intellectual refreshment over a 'gasper' in the school yard, it was Dick

(above and below)
Broken in two by the high seas the *Hindlea* comes to her last resting place on the cliffs at Moelfre. The tangled wreck is a tourist sight to this day (*Daily Mail*)

(above)
Dick Evans and the crew of the *Nafsiporos* celebrating their rescue with him (*Liverpool Daily Post & Echo*)

(below)
W McGuire, W J Adams, Oskar Rall, Mrs K Roberts and C Stocks having a cup of tea in the congregational chapel, Moelfre, Anglesey, after being rescued from the *Hindlea* (*Liverpool Daily Post & Echo*)

who was left in charge of the class. By and large the arrangement worked well. It only really fell down the morning the headmaster took an hour off to get married. The class was aware that something unusual was afoot when the headmaster arrived for morning prayers wearing a red bow tie. There was no other departure from his customary dress, but the red bow tie was somehow significant. It transpired that Mr Edwards, for many years a bachelor, was to be married that day to the headmistress of another village school three miles along the coast.

He left the class in Dick's charge. It was a mistake. That Saturday Dick had spotted an overladen apple tree on a smallholding outside the village. After giving the lessons out, he picked five special cronies and set off for the orchard. They were identically dressed in navy cord trousers, navy jerseys and the 4in deep white rubber collars, easily washed and dried, which were essential wear for country schoolboys. With string tied round their waists and their jerseys knobbly with stolen apples, they were just creeping out of the orchard when they saw the owner, John Parry, standing by the gate with Jim, his big, black dog.

'If you move an inch . . . ,' he thundered,' I set Jim on you.'

Terrified, the six boys were marched back to school with Jim snarling in the rear. They were standing in a guilty line, waiting, when the headmaster returned from his wedding.

'What's the trouble, Mr Parry?'

'I caught them stealing my apples, sir.'

'All right, Mr Parry. You go home and tend to your work. I'll see to this.'

The guilty six were kept behind when the class was dismissed. A wait and then the headmaster ordered them to unfasten the string round their waists. The boys stood shamefaced as apples poured from their jerseys, bouncing on the floor. Another wait. Then slowly Mr Edwards walked down the line, kicking apples from his path. When he came to Dick he stopped and looked through his eyes into, it seemed to the boy, his very soul.

'Richard,' he said. 'Oh, Richard. And on my wedding day too!'

Feeling more guilty than at any time in his life Dick waited for his punishment. The headmaster, however, had a fine instinct for torture.

'Go home,' he said. 'I'll deal with you in the morning.'

Dick spent the evening in apprehension in case his parents learned of his crime and that night he hardly slept at all. The next morning the beating came as a light relief.

Mr Edwards used every weapon he could find to capture the imagination of his pupils. Old sea captains in the village were persuaded to instruct the headmaster in navigation so that he in turn could give the boys at least one lesson they would enjoy. Through poems about the sea he tried to kindle their interest in literature and was not unsuccessful. One of his pupils, Hugh Griffiths, became a distinguished actor and Dick can still remember a poem he first read more than sixty years ago. It is, predictably, about lifeboats.

> Now to the rescue, launch the boats, I
>   see a drifting speck,
> Some straggler may be still aboard, some
>   sailor on the decks.
> Ply the oar, put from the shore and board
>   the bounding wreck.

Lifeboats had a special magic for the boys. They watched eagerly for distress signals from boats caught in the north-westerly gales. A flag at half-mast; sometimes a red ensign hoisted upside-down or, at night, a bucket of paraffin-soaked clothing tied to a spar and set alight were the conventional signals for help. Then it was a race to get to the lifeboat station to see the maroons going up.

The life-jackets of the full-time members of the crew and the bowman, the second coxswain and the coxswain were kept in the boat; but the twelve 'waistcoats' for the volunteers hung on pegs inside the station. As the boys watched, the village suddenly erupted with the pounding of feet as men came tumbling out of every cottage, eager to grab a waistcoat. There was fierce competition for the honour of a place in the lifeboat.

Everything stopped when the maroons went up even—if it happened to be a Sunday—services in the chapel. Dick has never forgotten those days:

> Chapel was crammed full. Every seat occupied on a Sunday night, sometimes with a strange preacher there from the country. And all of a sudden the maroons go up. In the days of the pulling and sailing lifeboats you wanted fifteen for a crew and you had four helpers on the slip. So there would be about twenty-five or thirty men wanting to get out, you see. You can imagine the scramble. And the poor minister sometimes in the middle of his sermon. What could he do? Only say, 'Amen'. And the children too, they wanted to rush out and watch the lifeboat. This happened very, very often on a Sunday night.

Once, on the way to school, the children saw the *Ellen Harrison* coming under sail past Moelfre Island. Her skipper, a giant they called Uncle Tom, was a special favourite. Halfway round she would not go on the other tack and ran aground on the rocky shore. School forgotten, the boys did an about-turn and ran back down the hill to the lifeboat station where they watched the launch.

'Very tricky,' pronounced Dick, knowledgeably. 'They won't be able to anchor because of the rocks.'

'Bet they will,' a voice challenged.

'They'll never save the *Ellen,*' another opined. 'Wonder what her cargo is?'

They saw the crew being taken off and later a flotilla of small boats put out to rescue her cargo of slate tiles. The boys earned a share of the salvage money by carrying the slates up the beach on stretchers they made from two poles with a cross-lattice of canvas.

Every youngster longed for the day when he could enter Mary Jones' toffee shop. No one under the age of fourteen was allowed inside. Not especially luxurious, with a long settle at one end and an oak counter at the other, it nevertheless hinted at the voluptuous life of the mariner. It was the preserve of the 'Homeward Bounders', the ships' boys on leave, too young to join their older shipmates in the local inn. Only feet that had trod a moving deck and those of their sweethearts in the village ever clattered down the four steps into the cellar shop where Mary sold cigarettes, sweets and tobacco. At night up to twenty cabin boys and teenage seamen sat with their girl friends on the settle, smoking away, drinking lemonade and yarning of strange adventures in far-off parts—Connahs Quay, Point of Air and Liverpool. It was the pleasant custom of the house for a 'Homeward Bounder' to treat all present to a bottle of lemonade and a bar of chocolate—both could be bought for a penny halfpenny—a gesture which could cost him as much as a florin.

The conventions were strictly observed by Mary Jones. Should the girl friend of one of her members who was absent at sea go about with another boy, Mary took it upon herself to report the flirtation to the sailor on his return.

One Sunday, when he was almost fourteen, Dick was admitted a member of the chapel. The next day a little ship, the *Daisy*, came into the bay and Dick, with a snow-white kitbag over his shoulder and a wave to his mates, climbed on board and became at last a sailor bound for far-off

Preston with a cargo of hay. With his kitbag stored in the fo'c's'le, ignored by the rest of the crew, Dick wandered round the deck for a while, growing more despondent every moment. Then, after the ship cast off and Moelfre disappeared over the horizon, he crept among the hay stacked in the hold and cried his eyes out.

3

ORDINARY SEAMAN

When Dick shipped out of Moelfre at the end of World War I an ordinary seaman was paid £2 a week and had to provide his own food. Not even bedding was supplied by the company. The seamen could not afford tailor-made cigarettes. They shook tobacco dust from their pockets, mixed it with tea leaves dried in the oven and rolled the mixture in newspaper.

The coasters of those days were called 'puffers'—the name was the only friendly thing about them. The fo'c's'le of the *Daisy*, where the crew of four ate, slept and relaxed, was a stinking, iron pit, the bulkheads dripping with sea water. There was so little room that when two men wanted to get dressed the others had to stay in their bunks. Twelve iron steps led down to the fo'c's'le; it was lit by a single oil lamp which was extinguished the first time the bow plunged in a heavy sea, leaving the crew in pitch darkness. The portholes were half covered in paint and daylight came in flashes like headlights. When the bow dipped, Dick could see nothing but green sea and wondered if she would ever come up again. The crew's food was cooked in a small stove wedged between the bunks and when, in rough seas, this could not be lit, the men went hungry until the ship was weather-bound under the shelter of land and they could indulge in massive bacon fry-ups.

There was no wheel-house on the *Daisy*; in the first minute of his watch the man on the wheel was drenched and soaking. The men took an hour about on the wheel, followed by an hour on stand-by, huddled over the steam boiler for warmth.

Reliefs were expected to arrive on the minute, and delay was repaid with interest by the next man. Towards the end of the four-hour watch, it was an effort to stay awake. Wet and exhausted, Dick stumbled back into the fo'c's'le to bedding soaked from the leaking porthole. This punishing schedule went on for several days at a time.

When Dick first told his parents he wanted to go to sea his mother had tried to prevent him, but his father felt it would be better to let him go. 'One trip will put him off,' he prophesied.

But, amazingly, Dick loved every moment of his new hard life. Knowing little English—everyone in his village spoke Welsh—he could hardly understand a word that was said by his new shipmates, two Irishmen and a Scot.

Dick had never been farther from home than Bangor and the first sight of Preston stunned him. If the sea held no terrors for him at fourteen, the bustling city did and, when the *Daisy* docked, he refused to go ashore. He was afraid he would get lost in the miles of mean streets round the docks and never find his way back.

If a coaster arrived in port on a Friday night, her crew was put on half pay until Monday when the next cargo was loaded. At every major port hundreds of unemployed seamen stood at the dock gates waiting to take the place of any crewman foolhardy enough to object to the owner's terms. Nevertheless the life fascinated Dick. He wanted to know everything about the *Daisy*. The work abroad presented no difficulty to the young boy. He had studied ships since he could walk. He could manage a ship's wheel and take his turn in any sea. When the others went ashore, he was content to stay aboard to clean the brasses which were green and pitted with salt.

From Preston the *Daisy* went to Garston where they loaded coal for Ireland. But, once again, when she docked in Waterford, the size of the place terrified him. For six months, while they traded between Ireland and Liverpool, Dick refused to go ashore.

One Saturday, when the ship docked in Garston, for the first time Dick felt homesick. His request for leave was refused. 'You're not going home,' the captain told him. 'I'm promoting you able seaman next week.'

An able seaman at fourteen and a half! This was something he had not expected for several years. His pay soared to £4 15s a week. Out of this he would have to send his mother £2, pay for an insurance stamp and his keep; he would be broke every Wednesday, but he did not mind. He was an able seaman.

In 1921, now aged sixteen and on leave from his coaster, Dick was taken on as a member of the Moelfre lifeboat crew. When the maroons went up, he rushed down with the other volunteers to the boat-house. The coxswain, Captain Lewis, was one man short and, seeing Dick standing head and shoulders above the other boys, he beckoned him over. 'Will you volunteer for a waistcoat?'

Dick was in the boat almost before the coxswain had finished speaking. There was a chorus of protest from the grizzled and bearded veterans who made up the crew. 'He's a bloody boy,' called one.

The coxswain silenced him. 'He'll do for me,' he said, motioning Dick to an oar and giving the winchman the order to let go the boat.

The *Charles and Eliza Laura* slid through the door and plunged into the white water at the foot of the slipway. Dick gasped as the bow torpedoed in, lurched sideways for a moment and then burst out of the sea like a porpoise surfacing.

In the bobbing boat the older men dropped the 4ft steel centreboard and raised the mast to break out the sail. There was a snag and the men cursed, their excitement bursting out in spurts of anger. The 'round hole', a steel ring which held the foresail spar, was jammed at the masthead. Valuable minutes would be lost in lowering the mast to release it so that the sail could be hoisted. Dick was on his feet in a moment. 'I'll get it.' Before anyone could stop him, he had shinned up the 20ft mast, freed the round hole and slid back to the deck.

There was a chuckle from the coxswain at the tiller. 'Sometimes boys can be very useful,' he said.

The 34ft pulling and sailing boat needed a crew of fifteen. There were twelve oars—blue on the port side and white on the starboard side; the coxswain could manoeuvre the boat by calling out the colour. The other three men were needed to trim the heavy canvas sails as they beat against the wind.

There was a 10-knot gale in the bay and, with the sails straining and the cable of the sea anchor streaming out behind, they climbed waves, hung poised, on the crest, gunwales deep in spray, and then pitched into the trough below. There was no shelter on the *Laura*. Dick sat clutching his shipped oar, feeling the icy water trickling down his neck, but the discomfort bothered him not at all. He thought back to his schooldays and the games he had played with other boys on the shore. Their 'lifeboat' had been an orange-box bought from the grocer for a shilling which they had earned selling firewood. For oars they used poles. It was always the same sailing ship they rescued—a hollowed-out rock shaped roughly like the hull of a boat; this they rigged meticulously with broomstick masts and driftwood spars. Dick was a real lifeboatman now.

They had been called to the aid of a three-masted schooner. Her skipper had two anchors out, but it would not be long before the heavy chains snapped and the ship was left completely at the mercy of the weather.

About 200 yards to windward of the schooner, Captain

Lewis ordered his crew to drop anchor and lower the sails. The 100-fathom anchor cable was played out, every man lending a hand as it raced past him. If the coxswain had judged the distance accurately, the anchor cable, fully stretched, would bring them just under the ship. An error of judgement on his part would fetch the lifeboat up short and an exhausting haul on the heavy, sea-soaked cable would be needed to bring up the anchor so that the whole exercise could begin again. But Captain Lewis had judged exactly and soon they were under the ship.

On the deck 10ft above, eight men in blue jerseys with grubby cravats wrapped round their necks clutched at the handrails looking down anxiously at their rescuers. The bowman of the lifeboat scrambled forward; he was holding an 18in long baton with a 4lb weight attached and a thin line spliced to a much stronger cable. Shifting his feet like a boxer to steady himself and, judging his moment with precision, he threw the weighted baton across to the schooner. The lead weight, drawing the thin line upwards like a white snake, clattered on the schooner deck and the cord tautened.

'Haul up the cable,' the coxswain shouted through cupped hands. On the deck, the skipper waved and issued an order. Two of the crew left the rail and picked up the weight. Soon the narrow cord was drawn in, pulling after it the heavier cable. Meanwhile the lifeboat pitched and rolled in the heavy seas. One moment she was level with the schooner's deck and Dick could have reached out and touched hands with the seamen; the next she was down in a trough and the plimsoll line on the ship's side was above his head.

The younger, more agile members of the schooner's crew were able to climb over the rails, hang for a moment and then, as the lifeboat came level, step to safety. Some—less nimble, or perhaps more frightened—jumped wildly and landed in a heap, sometimes in a tangle of arms and legs.

Dick was kicked on the head by a flailing leather sea boot. The last man to jump fell between the wooden walls of the schooner and the pitching lifeboat. If he escaped drowning, his head could be smashed like a nut when the two vessels were thrown together. Fortunately he surfaced just as a wave pushed the lifeboat away. Two of the crew grabbed him and, with an upward tug, threw him into the well of the boat behind them.

All hands hauled on the anchor cable. Aided only by a small winch, it was gruelling work to pull the lifeboat 200 yards through a heavy sea. It took four men to coil the 4in thick, soaking, salt-caked cable. Dick's hands were chafed and bleeding. At last they were back over the anchor. Dick was able to rest, while the masts were raised and the sails set. Against an offshore wind, the return trip took almost five hours but eventually they reached the comparative shelter of the headland. Dick could see men on the beach launching a 14ft tender. Soon it was alongside, taking off the crew of the schooner. Then it was his turn; blisters were beginning to balloon on his hands, his back throbbed where the oar of the man behind him had smashed into him as they rowed, and he had never been so cold. When he stepped out of the boat, the land seemed to pitch up and down. Above the high-water mark a group of schoolboys stood watching him and suddenly Dick felt marvellous. Their eyes, glowing with envy and hero-worship, warmed him more than any fire. With a new quiet dignity, he let himself be led to the chapel vestry and accepted an offering of hot buttered toast. Captain Lewis nodded to him over a mug of sweet tea. 'We'll look for you next time, Richard,' he said.

There was still work to be done after the rescue. Every item of equipment, the cable, the life-jackets, the boat itself had to be washed clean of salt, and the ropes coiled so that they would run freely the next time the maroons went up. Every month an RNLI inspector came to check the gear, and woe-betide coxswain and crew if everything was not shipshape.

In time Dick, nineteen and big for his age, moved from the *Daisy* to the *Cornish Coast*. In his spare time off-watch a massive Russian, who had joined the ship with Dick, taught him to box. In Llanelli, Dick and his Russian friend were drawn by the lights to a travelling fair. Neither of them had a penny to spend, but they were happy enough wandering round the sideshows. A crowd outside a boxing booth attracted their attention. Three bruisers stood on a raised platform in front while a barker harangued the onlookers.

'Anyone who can stand three rounds with my champion goes home with £5,' he promised, and he waved over his head a white £5 note, the first Dick had ever seen. It was more than a week's wages. For a moment Dick did not realize he had become the focus of attention. Then he saw the barker was pointing a stick at him.

'You're a big, strapping fellow,' he heard him say. 'Wouldn't you like to take on one of my lads?'

Dick was shocked at the thought. All those years of chapel upbringing revolted at the idea of going into a boxing ring. His mother would be furious. He shook his head violently.

'Afraid of him, are you?' the barker taunted him.

'Oh no, I'm not,' he shouted back, feeling an upsurge of his Welsh blood. The barker threw the staff he had been waving and Dick reached out automatically and caught it.

'You've done it now,' the Russian whispered. 'That means you've accepted the challenge.'

Bemused and embarrassed, Dick was pushed forward and found himself on the platform, dodging a storm lamp which hissed over his head.

Inside the booth the Russian caught up with him. 'The

other two were bad enough,' he warned, 'but you've taken on the champion.'

It was too late to back out. Dick shrugged his shoulders and, looking much more confident than he felt, climbed into the ring. His opponent, a huge negro, stood in his corner, powerful arms folded across a deep-barrelled chest. Dick remembered when a negro had once been brought ashore with the crew of a wrecked sailing ship. Black men were unknown in his part of Wales. The villagers were terrified until the minister had reassured them. He looked across the ring.

'He'll knock me down in a couple of seconds,' Dick thought. 'At least it won't last long.'

Wearing his dungarees and the rope-soled canvas shoes he had made himself, Dick held out his hands for the promoter to fit his boxing gloves. Now that the die was cast his nervousness left him and, when the bell went for the first round, he was quite calm.

The negro shot out of his corner. In the first flurry of punches, blood spurted from Dick's nose and his lip was badly cut. But when the round ended he was still on his feet.

Back in his corner his Russian shipmate was jubilant, 'I think you hurt him,' he said.

Dick looked out of a rapidly closing eye. 'I'm damn sure he hurt me,' he said.

In the second round all the bells of Aberdovey were ringing in Dick's ears, but he remembered the Russian's advice. 'Go in and jab him with your left. Jab him as quickly as you can, then bring your right over.'

As the negro came forward Dick's left shot out, but when he brought over his right he missed his opponent completely. Off balance he sprawled towards the ropes. There was a flash as the other boxer bared his white teeth and then it seemed that an ammunition train exploded in Dick's ears. He had never been hit so hard in his life. The booth spun round over his head, blurred faces circled him, noise surged and receded like heavy seas. He grappled for the ropes to prevent himself falling, as the negro leaped in for the kill. Blows rained on Dick as he gasped for breath, his rope-soles slipping on the canvas. A wave of nausea swept over him.

'Only two more minutes,' he heard someone roaring at him. 'Don't go down.'

'Remember the fiver,' someone else yelled. But the money was unimportant. All that mattered in the sea of pain was that the black man should not put him down. Somehow he managed to stay on his feet until the bell brought the round to an end.

'Now listen,' instructed the Russian. 'Keep on punching. Don't give him a chance to hit you. This is what he's after. He's going to knock you out now.'

When the bell rang for the third round, Dick could hardly stand. Every bone in his body ached; blood was pouring from his mouth and nose. There was no science in his boxing, but he was fit and hard from five years at sea. Hardly knowing what he was doing he stood square in the centre of the ring and slogged it out, blow for blow with his opponent. At the end of the bout he was still on his feet. Even the barker congratulated him as he handed over the £5 note.

'Can you change it?' Dick asked, through swollen lips. 'Half of it goes to my shipmate.'

Somehow, guided by the Russian, Dick got back to his ship. The skipper, Captain Harris, was a friend of Dick's father. If his mother ever found out that her only son had been fighting in a boxing booth she would disown him for sure. Nor was there any question of his sister being proud of him for standing up to three rounds with a professional bruiser.

Dick went on the bridge to take the ship out of Llanelli harbour—a tricky manoeuvre in a narrow channel. It was not until they were out at sea that, in the dim light of the binnacle, Captain Harris noticed Dick's bloodied face. He peered at it closely. 'My God, what the hell's happened to you?'

'Fell down the fo'c's'le ladder, sir.'

'You look as though a building fell on you.'

Dick could hardly move his mouth.

'So you fell down the fo'c's'le ladder?' the captain asked.

'Yes sir,' Dick mumbled.

'You damned liar,' said the skipper. 'I was there. I watched it all. I was standing on my chair for the last minute. My God, if ever anybody earned a fiver you did tonight!'

The praise meant nothing to Dick. Only one thing mattered. 'Don't tell my father will you, sir?' he begged.

In 1927 the Moelfre lifeboat carried out the first of the spectacular rescues which were to make the station famous throughout the United Kingdom. Dick was away at sea and it was little consolation to him that Hugh Owen—his cousin, who was to be his companion in the boat until his retirement—took part in the heroic venture. When he came home, he listened enviously to Hugh's story.

On the afternoon of 28 October, the ketch *Excel*, carrying coal from Point of Air to her home port of Poole, in Dorset, got into difficulties in one of the worst gales of the century. Fifty volunteers, every able-bodied man in Moelfre answered the call when the maroons went up. After the fifteen crew were chosen, the *Charles and Eliza Laura* was launched under the command of the second coxswain, William Roberts, who was Dick's uncle. A long hard sail brought them to the *Excel* some miles off Point Lynas. She was anchored to a German steamer, but was waterlogged and sinking. Her three-man crew were clinging to the rigging, too exhausted to board the other vessel. As the lifeboat approached, a crewman leaned over the stern of the steamer and cut the *Excel* adrift. The sinking ketch moved sluggishly away at the mercy of gale and sea.

William Roberts could see that the three men on board were far beyond helping themselves. If they were to be rescued the lifeboat would have to go to them. There was only one desperate course open to him and Roberts knew that in taking it he would risk the lives of his entire crew. He would have to put the *Laura* on to the deck of the ketch.

With superb seamanship and courage, the lifeboatmen bent to their oars and pulled into a huge wave which lifted them right on to the plunging, heaving deck of the *Excel*. Before a second wave lifted them clear, they managed to pluck the three men from the rigging. They were only just in time. As they were swept away, the lifeboatmen looked back to see the *Excel* disappearing beneath the waves. A moment later the sinking ketch would have dragged them down. The lifeboat was in a perilous condition. Her bottom boards were stove in and she was filling with water. By a miracle her buoyancy cases were not holed, but badly damaged as she was she could make no headway against the gale. Her foresail was soon blown away in a savage gust which snapped the mast. All night the *Laura* drifted helplessly. It was bitterly cold in the open boat which was exposed to the lashing spray and the biting wind.

One of the survivors from the ketch, who had been badly injured in the wreck, died before nightfall. His body was passed along the boat and laid on the deck in one of the last remaining spaces above water. The crew did what they could to secure the corpse, but during the 'jack-lights' of the storm the stiffened body could be seen rolling with the boat.

William Roberts, lashed to the tiller, was concerned about his men, all of them suffering from exposure. His namesake, the oldest member of the crew, was growing desperately weak as the night wore on. A sixty-three-year-old grandfather, he had been among the first to claim a waistcoat and

An aerial picture of the *Nafsiporos* in the moments before the Moelfre and Holyhead lifeboats made their first rescue runs (*Daily Express*)

The rescue is over. Ten lives have been saved and the effort it cost is written in every line on Dick's face. The photograph was taken after the *Nafsiporos* rescue (*Radio Times*)

a place in the boat. His thinner blood made the older William Roberts particularly vulnerable to the penetrating cold. Just before dawn, his head fell forward and he died.

After thirteen hours at sea they managed to drop anchor near Puffin Island. The keeper of the Penmon light saw them and summoned the Beaumaris lifeboat. The *Laura* was taken in tow and brought safely to Beaumaris. Among the crowd at the slipway was Hugh Griffiths, then a schoolboy. Years later, when he had become well known for his film appearances, he recalled the lifeboat's return: 'It was the first time I had seen dead men. It was only then I realized just what being a lifeboatman meant and the appalling risks they took to go to the aid of others.'

Second coxswain William Roberts had spent thirteen hours at the tiller, fighting the sea. He was blind when they brought him ashore, and did not recover his sight for seventeen hours. Both he and Owen Jones—a sea captain who was acting second coxswain—received the RNLI's gold medal. The bronze medal was awarded posthumously to lifeboatman William Roberts, as well as a small pension for his grandchild. Twelve other members of the crew, including Dick's cousin, Hugh Owen, received bronze medals and citations on vellum. Colonel Lawrence Williams, the village squire who was the much revered secretary of the Moelfre boat for half a century, was presented with a barometer.

One of the members of that brave crew was old Tom Williams. He had rounded Cape Horn in sailing ships and, in his retirement, he returned to Moelfre. One day, while tending his nets, he saw a sailing boat in difficulties. He put out in his own boat and saved the occupants, a man and his wife who had been washed overboard.

Back on the beach, the rescued man was briskly grateful. 'Now, my man,' he said. 'What do I owe you?'

Tom was shocked. 'Owe me? You owe me nothing. I'm a lifeboatman. We don't take money for saving life.'

'But, look here,' the man insisted. 'You must have something. You saved my wife.'

Old Tom was silent for a moment. 'All right,' he said. 'Give me what you would have given me the moment before I plucked you out of the sea.'

Promotion came quickly on the 'puffers'. Before he was twenty, Dick was second mate and later, chief officer. His ships traded mostly to tiny Irish ports with colourful names: Klonakiltie, Kinsale, Youghal, Casavein, Bearhaven and Dingle. Soon there was not a port in Ireland Dick had not visited. A Celt from a Welsh village, he felt an immediate rapport with the Gaelic-speaking inhabitants. During the Troubles of the 1920s, when English seamen set foot ashore at their peril, Dick was always welcome and free to wander round the ports at will.

In 1926, at the height of the Troubles, terrorists blew up every bridge from Cork to Limerick and trains and buses ceased to run. Trade between the two towns was at a standstill until Dick's 'puffer' was chartered by the government. It was dangerous work. Often, in port, the crew had to shelter in the fo'c's'le while gun battles were going on. Afterwards curfews were imposed and sentries posted everywhere, ready to shoot at any movement. Dick, a neutral Welshman, was allowed ashore to buy supplies for himself, but was forbidden to take any food aboard for his shipmates. Two of his Welsh friends were going ashore from another ship when they were challenged by a sentry. 'Friend,' replied one.

The other, an old man from Moelfre, tugged at his sleeve. 'Tell him "friends", for God's sake. There's two of us!'

At these Irish ports, Dick spent his free evenings in little shops where he drank lemonade sitting on a settle before a kitchen fire. If he was lucky he would be invited to share the supper the regular customers were given every night. In a cauldron over the fire, the shopkeeper's wife boiled potatoes in their jackets and a pig's head. The broth from the head gave the potatoes an exquisite flavour. After supper there would be a sing-song with the pretty Irish village girls. The postal service between the coastal towns had ceased to operate and, for the price of a stamp, Dick undertook to carry letters between these girls and their boyfriends along the coast. For the first time in his service, he earned a little pocket money.

On board the coaster, private business flourished. The passengers, mostly wealthy cattle dealers, would become desperately sick from the motion of the vessel. Renting them a bed in the fo'c's'le was a rewarding venture for the crew, and the chief engineer, justly called 'Cash', made a handsome profit selling them coffee at twopence a cup.

Dick's sailing routine was from Liverpool to Ireland, then up the Scottish lochs for cargoes of timber from the Highland forests. There were no charts, the ship's boat had to be put over the side so that one of the crew could row over to the loch-side villages to ask the way. Loading the timber took up to four days. Logs were dragged through the forest by a cable from the ship's winch, floated to the ship and slung into the hold. When the hold was full, additional logs were stacked on deck.

Sometimes they took on a cargo for France. But, unless they were bound for Brittany, where the local language has many similarities with Welsh, Dick was less interested in the destination than in the time it would take to load and unload. At sea, time was divided into four-hour watches; for him, the luxury of an undisturbed night's sleep in dock was more attractive than the most romantic port of call.

Life at sea was not without drama. Dick, chief officer by now on the MV *Colin* bound for Westport, Southern Ireland, with a cargo of coal. One night, as the Tusker lighthouse loomed out of the darkness, he thought he heard groaning from the captain's cabin below.

'You'd better go and see what's wrong,' Dick told a seaman.

The man was soon back. 'Quick. I think he's killed himself. There's blood all over.'

Dick lifted the telegraph to ring for the engine room. The second engineer came up and together they went to the cabin. The captain was alive but in a very bad way.

'The nearest port is Rosslare. I'll make for that,' said Dick. But there were no charts in the drawer for that part of the Irish coast and he dare not risk taking the ship blind through those rocky coastal waters. Happily a fishing boat hove into sight and the skipper agreed to guide them in and radio for a doctor. The captain was found to have peritonitis and was taken to hospital.

Dick had orders to take the ship on to Waterford. It was his first command. The *Colin* then proceeded to Wales to pick up a cargo of stone for Manchester. At Garston Dick expected to find his replacement, but no one was there. He rang the owner to find out when the relief would be arriving.

'We should have one for the next trip, if you can take charge of this one,' he was told. 'No hurry, surely? You're doing a marvellous job.'

There was no skipper waiting at Westport, nor at Ayr in Scotland where they loaded coal for St Brion, in France; nor at St Brion, Newlyn, Newhaven, Liverpool or Bray. Dick was getting farther from home with every trip. He was carrying out the work of both skipper and first officer, which meant that he was up day and night. For this he was paid a first officer's wage of £5 a week.

At last the new skipper arrived. He was an old man who had served in sailing ships all his life. 'I understand you've been captain of this ship for the past six weeks,' he said.

'Yes, sir.'

'I'm going to rely a great deal on you,' the skipper said. 'I've never been in a steamship before. When we take her out, you go on the bridge and I'll go on the fo'c's'le head. You can show me how to handle her when we get to sea.'

The new captain was a first-class navigator, but the steam engine was an unknown quantity to him. So Dick, accepting the situation philosophically, went back to the bridge. The passage was once again to Scotland to load timber. It was winter and the mountains were covered in thick snow. When loading was finished, the captain would not hear of moving. 'The weather's closing in,' he said.

'We'll be all right if we keep to the centre of the loch,' Dick argued. 'There's plenty of water. We must be in Garston, discharging, the day after tomorrow.'

But it was four days later when they arrived in Garston. The owner was waiting on the dockside and the captain was dismissed.

So, at the age of twenty-three, Dick became master of the MV *Colin*, 320 tons. 'Salt-caked coaster' she may have been, but in Dick's eyes the *Mauretania* was not fit to sail in the same sea.

He was not to enjoy his command for very long. His uncle, John Matthews, had been offered the full-time job of coxswain of the Moelfre lifeboat. Someone was needed to take over his butcher's shop in the village and the family decided that Dick was the obvious choice.

He was thunderstruck. As captain of the *Colin*, he had achieved his ambition to be master of his ship years before he could reasonably have hoped to do so. The idea that he should give it up to serve scrag-end to the village women was unthinkable. Dick started to write a letter of protest, but somehow the words would not come and after the sixth attempt he gave up.

On his next leave, he explained his views face to face with his family. His mother, as always, was severely practical.

'It's a marvellous opportunity,' she argued. 'You will be your own boss. And the money is much better than you get at sea.'

'The money doesn't matter. I don't care about money. I'm a ship's captain just as I've dreamed of being all my life. I love that ship.'

Back in Liverpool the owner took his mother's part.

'You must go home,' he said. 'See how things work out. If you don't like the job you can always come back.'

There was nothing for it. Sadder than he had ever been in his life Dick bade a gloomy goodbye to the *Colin* and became the village butcher. The only consolation was that he would have a permanent place in the lifeboat crew.

'I look bloody ridiculous,' he told the mirror in his bedroom, when he put on his striped apron for the first time.

Serving behind the counter was even worse than he imagined. In his desperation he took £10 out of the first week's takings and hid it, hoping to prove that the business was not worth bothering about, so that he could go back to sea. But the family insisted that he stay.

Dick had much to learn. Selling meat was the easiest part of the job of a country butcher. In those days cattle and lambs were bought on the hoof, driven back to the village to be slaughtered, and the carcasses cut up at the back of the shop.

Dick's first visit to the market at Llanerchymedd was a disaster. The regulars eyed him with a suspicion which grew to frank distrust when he started to bid. Until then the bidding had risen in a stately fashion from the ridiculously low, in the opinion of the auctioneer, to the ruinously high, in the eyes of the assembled butchers. Dick had little time for such niceties. When he saw a pen of sixty lambs that seemed to him to be worth £1 a head he bid that amount, thus robbing the auction of all its excitement.

He was drawn on one side by a butcher from another village. 'You're taking all the art out of it, young man,' he complained. 'Start at 17s and move with the crowd, boy. Bloody Smithfield it is, not Monte Carlo.'

Obediently Dick fell in with the customary practice of this new club of which he had become, unwillingly, a member.

'Seventeen and three,' said a butcher.

'Seventeen and six,' said Dick, sighing audibly; he was rewarded with an approving nod from his instructor.

In the end the lambs still sold for £1 and Dick could see no sense in it all.

There were further complications when Dick met Nansi, a farmer's daughter from Anglesey. By the unwritten laws of the village, he should have married into the family of a sea captain or at least a chief engineer. But Dick overcame the objections and made her his wife.

He built up his butcher's business until he was killing a hundred lambs a week. To help him drive them the eight miles from market, he bought two sheepdogs. Scott and Twm were splendid workers. In Llanerchymedd, Dick would take up his position in front of the flock, with Twm at his side and Scott bringing up the rear. He could then walk home reading the penny magazine he had bought, without ever looking up. Everything was safely left to the two dogs.

World War II brought further disillusionment for Dick. He had been used to selling only top-quality meat. It appalled him to have to sell what was sent to him by the Ministry of Food and he felt obliged to look for alternative suppliers. One Monday afternoon, Dick decided to go foraging. At the Menai Bridge market, where he hoped no one knew him, he bought a pig. By 9.30 it had been slaughtered and was hanging in the shop ready to be cut up the next morning. He was just getting ready for bed when there was a knock at the door. It was the government inspector.

'Mr Evans? I believe you were in the Menai Bridge market today and bought a pig?'

Dick decided to put his cards on the table. 'I did,' he admitted. 'It's in the slaughter-house ready to be cut up in the morning.'

'We know all about it,' the inspector said. 'Look now, you've been very honest. Provided you get rid of it by 9 o'clock I'm going to forget all about it. You're a decent fellow. I don't like informers and the dirty way you've been reported.'

In the morning Dick was out in his van at first light. He drove to a smallholding where he knew a mother of three children was having a difficult time eking out her rations. When she saw the cuts of pork she could not believe her eyes. 'Oh God,' she said, 'my husband loves a pork chop.'

'How many do you want?'

'Do you mean it? Could we have one each?'

'As long as you're quick, you can have as many as you like. You wouldn't like a joint as well, would you?'

On another occasion, when Dick was stopped by a Ministry of Food inspector, he had six 'unauthorized' lambs in his van. To drown their bleating, he revved heavily on the accelerator.

'It's my starter,' he explained. 'I daren't let the engine stop. I'd never get it going again.'

The inspector was dubious. 'I see,' he said. 'You carry on then. But I'll see you at the slaughter house.'

Dick's brother-in-law, on leave from the army, was waiting to help him slaughter the lambs. Everything had been prepared. The cradle to hold the lambs, the buckets for the blood, and the killing knives were all laid out and there was no time to put them away.

'Get this van out of here,' Dick begged. 'I don't care where you go. Just drive anywhere till the coast is clear.'

When the inspector arrived he looked suspiciously at the equipment. 'Slaughtering, are you?' he asked.

Dick was scornful. 'What have I got to slaughter? This is just to remind me of the times when I could kill my own beasts and give my customers what they wanted. I always leave it exactly like this.'

The inspector was sympathetic. 'Never mind,' he said. 'One day you'll be doing it again.'

4

MASTER OF A COASTER AND WORLD WAR II

Dick's uncle John, the lifeboat cox, was not a tall man nor did he give the appearance of strength, but he was as brave as a lion and the finest swimmer in the village. One blustery winter day, with a south-westerly gale blowing straight off the snow-covered Caernarfon mountains, he was at home when word came that the lifeboat had slipped its mooring and was being washed out on to the rocks. Grabbing his cap and scarf, and pulling on his waterproof greatcoat, he ran down the street to the headland. A group of old seamen were standing on the cliff edge. 'Too late,' they shouted. 'She's well out. Look!'

The empty lifeboat, some 400 yards out on a pitching sea, was being borne rapidly towards the rocks. Still in his cap, scarf, greatcoat and sea boots, Matthews dived 30ft from the cliff top into the boiling sea.

'Bloody fool's committed suicide,' one of the watchers said, plainly echoing the view of the others. John Matthews, then a man in his fifties, had apparently done just that. Then someone caught sight of his cap floating away. The crowd fell silent until one of them noticed that it was in fact moving against the tide. To their astonishment, Matthews was swimming strongly towards the drifting lifeboat. Yard by yard, he moved closer to it until he was able to grab a sheet, pull himself inboard and drop the anchor before the boat hit the rocks which would have ripped her to pieces.

The RNLI was at a loss to find an appropriate recognition

for such a staggering feat. Medals were awarded for saving life; there was no precedent for rescuing a lifeboat. In the end John Matthews was presented with a gold watch—the only time such an award was made by the RNLI. During his thirty-eight years as coxswain, he collected three silver medals, two bronze and several 'thanks on vellum'. These he hardly ever showed, but he was particularly proud of the gold watch and could easily be persuaded to display it.

Dick's uncle knew every trick of tide, every rock, every haven on the coast round Moelfre. His mind was a chart-room of the seas between the village and the Isle of Man, but he had never been out of his own district in his life. The first time his crew saw anything like apprehension cross his face was in 1930 when he was instructed to collect a new boat from the Isle of Wight. The return passage did not worry him, but the thought of travelling through London on the underground train filled him with dread.

The pulling and sailing boats, which had done such wonderful service since the nineteenth century, were being replaced by petrol-engined boats of a new design. The *George Wade* was to be the first of these to come to Anglesey. John Matthews, with Dick as bowman, three other crewmen and a mechanic—a new role in the lifeboat service—set off for Cowes to collect it. The taxi drive from Moelfre to Bangor passed without incident, but the train journey, the first Dick's uncle John had ever made, was for him less pleasurable. In London amid the scurrying tube travellers, Matthews was completely disorientated. By the time the party had dropped to platform level at the Euston underground station, he was no longer a creature of independent will. Swept along by the flow of humanity, Matthews was carried into a tube train ahead of his crew. Before he could get his bearings the doors closed on him. The others fought through the crowd in time to see their coxswain, face pressed to the glass and arms waving madly, disappearing out of the station, shouting 'Open this door!' They took the next train and, one station down the line, found their coxswain a stricken and angry man. Goodwill was not restored until, arriving in Portsmouth, Matthews heard the harsh, reassuring cry of seagulls.

At Cowes, as soon as he was shown the new lifeboat, the *George Wade*, he was a man transported. The crew had scarcely time for a meal before their coxswain was hurrying them back to the slipway to get the *GW* out to sea.

The passage to Moelfre took five days in appalling weather, but Matthews was imperturbable. It was only when he thought of the London tube that he shuddered. The *GW* came through mountainous seas, lashed by rain and buffeted by full gales. From Cowes to Brixham, Brixham to Falmouth, Falmouth to Penzance, Penzance to Newlyn, Newlyn across the Bristol Channel to Fishguard, Fishguard to Holyhead, Holyhead to Moelfre, they met every sea imaginable.

The arrival at Moelfre of its first motor lifeboat was a cause of celebration. As soon as she was sighted crossing Red Wharf Bay everyone lined the cliffs to watch. A reception committee, led by the lifeboat secretary Colonel Williams, was waiting on the slipway.

'What sort of a passage d'ye have, Matthews?' asked the Colonel as they came ashore.

'Quiet enough really, sir,' he said, and then the dark memory crossed his mind again. '*Arglwydd*, I'd forgotten. We were in a terrible disaster in the underground railway.'

The passing of the old pulling-and-sailing lifeboat *Charles and Eliza Laura* marked the end of an era. Sailing boats had been rescuing shipwrecked mariners long before the RNLI was formed. In 1772 Dr John Sharp, vicar of Bamburgh in Northumberland, became concerned at the number of wrecks on the coast near his parish and, in 1786, he commissioned his first rescue boat from a British coachbuilder, Lionel Lukin.

After the loss of HMS *Racehorse* off Longness, Isle of Man, in 1823 Sir William Hillary, a Douglas notable, published a pamphlet appealing for a national institution for the preservation of life at sea. A public meeting followed on 4 March 1824, and the National Institution for the Preservation of Life from Shipwreck was founded. There were already thirty-nine privately funded lifeboats in existence, and the £10,000 received in donations by the institution in its first year was used to buy another twelve. In 1824–5, 342 lives were saved. The organization became the Royal National Lifeboat Institution in 1854.

Anglesey's long tradition of lifeboat service was formalized in the eighteenth century when Frances Lloyd, a Caernarfon bluestocking, married James Williams, the rector of Llanfairynghornwy on the island. They had barely set up house after their honeymoon before they witnessed a terrible disaster. On a calm, clear day a packet-boat, *Alert*, struck the West Mouse rock off the coast near their home and began to break up. Of the 140 passengers and crew, only seven survived. Horrified at what they had seen, James and Frances Williams set about founding the Anglesey Lifeboat Association. The local gentry were canvassed for funds; and Frances made lithographs and sold them to raise money to buy lifeboats and reward rescuers. In a very short time the association's first lifeboat was riding at anchor in Cemlyn Bay.

When the *Active*, of Belfast, was breaking up at the mouth of the bay in weather too rough for the lifeboat to put to sea, the Rev. James—who always took an oar when the boat went out on rescues—managed to throw a grapnel into the ship's bowsprit shroud. This enabled a hook to be pulled over to the wreck and the crew was saved. His wife was no less resourceful; she would brave any sea to go over and nurse the men on the Skerries light when they fell ill.

By the time the Anglesey Association was taken over by the RNLI in 1856, the island's rescue service had saved over 400 lives. There had been a rescue boat at Moelfre since 1830; it had saved sixteen lives in two launches. Then the Cemlyn lifeboat was transferred there. This was replaced in 1867, when the London Sunday Schools Lifeboat fund provided a new one, the *London Sunday School and Charles Scone*. In 1874 there was another replacement—the *Lady Vivian*—bought from funds collected by Lady Vivian of Beaumaris. From 1884, when the *Lady Vivian* was taken out of service, two lifeboats were stationed in turn at Moelfre. Both called *Star of Hope*, they were gifts of Mrs Atherton Howard of Cheltenham. Their name had caught Dick's imagination as a boy. He could imagine how a sailor, shipwrecked and clinging for his life to a broken spar, would feel when he looked up and saw the name *Star of Hope* on the lifeboat.

In 1910 the last *Star of Hope* was replaced by the *Charles and Eliza Laura*, bought with the legacy of Mrs R. S. Clark, of London; twenty years later, she was going out of service. The pullers and sailers had a proud record. In 105 launches, the Moelfre lifeboats saved 309 lives.

Cox'n John Matthews, a reactionary, disliked boats with engines, but he had to admit that the *George Wade* greatly increased the Moelfre crew's rescue capabilities. They could extend their range and were not dependent on the wind. Despite her engine, the new boat was not perceptibly faster than the *Laura* had been. Five knots in a rough sea had been nothing to her twelve oarsmen. The difference was that the *GW* could maintain her speed all day. This provoked many an hour of pleasant argument. The coxswain would argue that his old crew at the oars could match the speed of the engines; the mechanic would reply that the engine could run all day at the same speed. Matthews always had the last word. 'Aye,' he would say, 'you maybe could, if the sea was made of petrol.'

The rough passage from Cowes had given Dick and the others in the crew an excellent chance to get the feel of the new boat and they were anxious to take her out on a service. On that coast they never had long to wait. The first was to a ketch in trouble off Cemaes Bay. Her sails had been blown away in a force 9 gale 8 miles north of Moelfre. When the *GW* came up it was obvious to coxswain and crew that had they been in *Laura* they would have been too late to save her. She was drifting at an alarming rate on to a rocky reef. Sailing dangerously near the rocks themselves, the lifeboat crew came under the ketch's stern. In her bows the *GW* carried a line-throwing gun. Dick, as bowman, prepared to send out the rope so that they could make fast to the ketch whilst the crew jumped into the lifeboat.

Seeing the line racing out and landing on the forward deck of the ketch, Cox'n Matthews suddenly realised the *GW* offered him a different course of action. The ketch was a wooden ship, heavily laden with a cargo of tiles, and she had shipped a great deal of water. A crash against such a solid obstacle might easily sink the lifeboat. Thanks to her engine power, however, there would be no need to sail under the drifting vessel.

'We'll tow her in,' Matthews said. 'Make the line fast to our stern.'

Towing was only marginally less risky than taking the crew off. By now the lifeboat was pitching alarmingly in the huge waves. Their passage to Holyhead took them on the notoriously dangerous seaward side of the Skerries. As the lifeboat approached, a strong ebbing tide pushed at her, nudging her nearer and nearer to the rocks. Her own power might counter the force of the tide, but the ketch dragging sluggishly behind them on the tow would be unable to offer any resistance.

'Shorten the tow,' Matthews shouted. 'And put out another line. Tell the ketch to make both lines fast, port and starboard amidships.'

Keeping the *GW* head on to wind and sea, playing the ketch like a kite, Matthews made the tide work for him. It was a long, grindingly slow passage, but at last, after ten anxious hours, they reached the safety of Holyhead harbour.

The next service was a severe test of the lifeboatmen's bravery. Fire is the most feared of all maritime hazards; taking a petrol-driven lifeboat alongside a blazing ship adds an extra dimension of danger. The schooner *Kate* was enveloped in flames when the *GW* came up on her stern. Coils of smoke poured from her holds, the rigging was burning fiercely and tongues of fire curled round her masts. As the lifeboat reached her, the hull was well alight; in every man's mind was the thought of the 80 gallons of petrol they carried. Cox'n Matthews could see that the fire was fiercest fore and aft where it had taken a firm hold on the cargo. Amidships, the flames appeared to be less intense. The schooner's crew were huddled in a circle of flame, not daring to jump for the sea itself seemed to be on fire.

Cox'n Matthews—who was standing above the fuel tank—steered the lifeboat unhesitatingly into the inferno. As the bow struck the schooner's side, the first of the crew jumped to safety. To carry out such a manoeuvre once was a triumph of courage and seamanship; Matthews took his boat into the flames three times. He did not leave the blazing schooner until his crew, kicking burning spars over the side and with flames singeing their hair, had helped every man off the fiery deck.

Back at the slipway the Moelfre women, as always, had hot food waiting in the chapel vestry for the survivors. The lifeboatmen were at last able to examine their craft. She was in a shocking state. All the paint of the bow had been

Donald Murley Francis who took over command as coxswain of the *Watkin Williams* following Dick's retirement. Tragically he died a year later following a short illness (*Daily Mirror*)

(above)
The Moelfre lifeboat the *Watkin Williams* during trials after repairs in the Menai Straits (*RNLI*)

(below)
The *Edmund and Mary Robinson* reserve lifeboat used in the rescue of the *Hindlea* (*RNLI*)

burned away and her timbers were charred. It was a miracle that the petrol tank had not exploded.

In the autumn of 1939, the submarine, *Thetis*, on sea trials from Cammel Laird's shipyards in Birkenhead, sank off Moelfre with the loss of all but four of her crew of 103. The lifeboat was not called out; there was no one to save. Salvage operations continued for several weeks. On shore Dick was among those who watched engrossed. The 4,000-ton *Sea Lion* was brought from Liverpool and rigged with balks of 18in-square timber athwart the ship. She took up station above *Thetis* while her divers made a cradle of wire cable under the submarine's keel. As the tide rose so did *Sea Lion*, lifting *Thetis* from the sea bottom. Progress was slow. Even though two tugs were towing her, *Sea Lion*, with the submarine slung under her, covered only three miles before the operation was suspended by the next low tide. When finally *Thetis* was raised to the surface in Moelfre Bay, the bodies were brought ashore and laid in rows in the lifeboat station. To the lifeboatmen, hardened to tragedy as they are, the sight of those fifty bodies laid out on the floor was sickening. They felt their own helplessness; there was nothing that they could have done, and this too sickened them.

Thetis was eventually beached on Traeth Bychan, below the village, patched up and finally towed back to Cammel Laird's for a refit. A year later, the submarine sailed again under a new name, HMS *Thunderbolt*. None of her crew knew of her sinister history. For three years, under the command of Lieutenant-Commander Bernard Crouch, DSO and Bar, she harried enemy shipping, sinking two U-boats and five supply ships. In the spring of 1943 she vanished and nothing more was heard of her—once again the submarine had been lost, this time with all hands.

At the outbreak of war Dick had been hoping to command a flotilla of torpedo boats to attack enemy coastal shipping, but Colonel Williams, the lifeboat secretary, had quashed the idea. 'You're needed here,' he said. So Dick found himself serving in two ways—as second coxswain of the lifeboat and as signals sergeant in the Home Guard.

Armed only with walking sticks Dick and another Home Guard stood on Traeth Bychan, on the lookout for Germans. While they waited, Dick recalled the night back in 1915 when his grandfather had heard the sound of 'shooting'. The people of Moelfre had been convinced that they would be the target of any German attack. There might, they thought, be preliminary skirmishes along the Western Front, but it was quite clear to them that the eyes of the Kaiser were turned upon Anglesey. There was therefore only one possible explanation for the noise that had awoken his grandfather. 'Submarines!' he roared, leaping out of bed and struggling into his trousers.

Dick, staying at his aunt's house that night, had also been woken up. 'There's a German submarine landed on the lifeboat slipway,' his aunt told him. 'You'd better get up.'

By the time young Dick was dressed and downstairs, the whole village was awake; people were scurrying from one house to another. The coastguards of the day—farmers who did voluntary duties as coast watchers and wore armbands bearing the initials 'CW'—toured the village turning out lights so that the submarine would not have an easy target.

'They've come to shoot us all,' Dick heard someone say.

He could also hear his aunt beseeching the Lord. She was a grand one for praying and He would be sure to listen to her. But when she reached the end, the boy realized with alarm that she was not saying a prayer for his safety but for his Uncle Hugh, at sea with the Merchant Navy. She was not in the least concerned about the submarine.

In this chaos, grandfather was a rock of calm determination.

'You take Kitty to the forest,' he told his wife. 'I'll stay and guard the cottage.'

As Dick's little sister hurried off clutching her grandmother's hand, she stole a look back. Her grandfather was standing squarely in the cottage door, brandishing a rolling-pin and waiting to knock out the first German who dared to walk up the path. But the noise was not a U-boat.

It was a fishing boat which had been blown noisily on and off the slipway that night. It was several years before the owner dared admit that his vessel had been the 'enemy submarine'. There were people in the village who would certainly have killed him.

Now, in another world war, Dick was guarding the beaches with a walking stick in his hand. He remembered his grandmother saying how silly Grandfather had been, expecting to stop a U-boat crew with a rolling pin. What would she have thought, if she had known that thirty years later her grandson in the Home Guard was expected to do the same thing with a walking stick?

'What *are* we going to do if a U-boat comes?' his companion asked.

'I don't know about you,' Dick replied firmly, 'but I'm going home.'

The Moelfre Home Guard platoon was made up almost entirely of retired sea captains, some of them of considerable age, and they found marching tiring and irksome. In due course they were supplied with weapons and on Sundays they went out on exercise fighting bloody mock battles in the countryside. At night, they guarded the road into Moelfre and every car had to be stopped. The veterans stood, bayonets fixed, in the centre of country lanes daring Hitler to do his worst. One night, on guard at the crossroads at the entrance to the village, Dick, with old Tom Williams at his side, waved a car down. The signal was ignored and, before Dick could stop him, Tom fired. There followed a loud screech of brakes. Dick could hear women sobbing in the car. Tom was not to be deterred. Covering the terrified occupants with his rifle, he said in the best Hollywood manner: 'Don't move. I won't miss next time.'

'It's you, Tom Williams,' a voice accused him. 'You ought to be ashamed. I thought it was the Germans.'

The Home Guard provided the men with light relief from the more demanding services of the lifeboat. On 28 January 1940, the men of the *GW* established a wartime record when they brought off the entire crew of sixty from ss *Gleneden*, of Glasgow. She had gone aground in a south-easterly gale on the Dutchman Bank, south of Puffin Island, at the mouth of the Menai Strait.

Gleneden was stuck hard and fast on the bank with waves breaking over her decks. Cox'n Matthews estimated there would be enough water at high tide to come alongside, although there was a risk that he too would run aground. At the first attempt the lifeboat took off forty-five men and somehow got them to Beaumaris where ambulances were waiting by the pier. On returning to the sandbank it was obvious to Matthews that *Gleneden* had been taking a terrible pounding and in a very short time would begin to break up. Dick, the second coxswain, was standing by the wheel when his uncle told him, 'You'll have to go aboard yourself, Richard.' The loud hailer was useless in the uproar of sea and gale. 'Tell the captain that unless he and his officers leave straight away there is nothing we can do for them.'

Towering above them in the darkness, *Gleneden* looked like an iron cliff. The rope-ladder was twisting violently in the wind and only with difficulty was Dick able to grab its flailing ends and haul himself on to the lowest rung. The climb up the ship's side was nerve-racking. Every time the ship rolled, the ladder moved away from her side only to crash back again, hammering Dick's knuckles against the metal. Several times he was on the point of falling into the sea below. At last he felt his arm grabbed and found himself in a circle of *Gleneden*'s officers. He passed on his uncle's message. The words were barely out of his mouth when the night erupted. He heard metal tearing apart and the violent snap of timber.

'She's breaking her back,' the captain said. Dick realized he was still reluctant to leave his ship and remembering his own feelings about the *Colin* he could sympathize. At last the captain made up his mind, motioned his officers to the ladder and finally went down himself. They were hardly under way in the lifeboat when *Gleneden* began to break up.

The tide was ebbing; there would not be enough water to bring the boat through the safer, narrow race south-east of Puffin Island. The outer passage on the north side had a greater depth of water, but was made hazardous by sand-banks and exposure to the breaking seas. Not until they were safely through was Dick able to ask the question that had been niggling at him all night. 'How the hell did you manage to run her aground?' he demanded of the chief officer beside him. 'The Dutchman's marked on the chart plainly enough. You must have been miles off course.'

In fact *Gleneden* had been torpedoed well out at sea, off Bardsey Island. Although she was badly holed, the pumps were getting rid of the water marginally faster than it was pouring in through the side. Her skipper decided to try for port and managed to reach Holyhead. It seemed possible he could make Liverpool but, halfway between Point Lynas and Holyhead, the pumps could no longer keep up with the flood of water. He radioed for instructions and was told to beach her on the nearest bank so that some of her cargo of iron ore could be salvaged. It was no accident as Dick had supposed; the beaching had been a skilful act of seamanship.

Dick, remembering those cold nights at sea, describes the wartime years in his own words:

During the war we found it extremely difficult to do rescue work with the lifeboat. The lighthouses on all the headlands had cut their beams to less than half their power and the frequency too was reduced. Point Lynas used to show a light every minute. Well, it was every ten minutes in the war. If you did miss the light it meant twenty minutes' wait and that is a long time to be blind in a heavy sea. And it was very easy to miss it. A lifeboat is very low in the water—it's not the same as being on the bridge of a ship.

Moelfre is on the main shipping lane for Liverpool and Manchester, and ships made for Point Lynas to embark or disembark their pilots. We had to be very careful; in these convoys there was quite a crowd of ships. They would have very dim lights and on the lifeboat we had no lights at all. We had to be looking all the time in case we hit one. To go out as we did—very, very often twenty-five miles into the Irish Sea—looking for a crashed plane with nothing to guide us was not easy. Unless the air crews we were looking for had flares, it was very difficult to find them in the pitch dark. Again, coming back after searching for two or three hours we had to fight the current. We'd be steering north and the tide going east to west would carry us off the line of our course. There were no leading lights, no lights on the houses to guide us; we relied on dead reckoning. The lifeboat did 7½ knots. If we were twenty-five miles out it should have been fairly simple to work out our course home. But we did not know we were twenty-five miles out. We could have been more, we could have been less; even half a point wrong would put us several miles out of our course.

Very often we had to stop the engines on the outward

passage to try to hear the airmen shouting. We'd be drifting for several minutes and the tide and the wind would take complete control, so it was very difficult for the cox'n to know how to set his course for Moelfre. Indeed on many occasions I wondered how the cox did find his way back because there are treacherous rocks on that coast. There is an island between Moelfre and Point Lynas, three miles from Moelfre Island, called Dulas Island and we always give it a wide berth going out because there are very nasty rocks all round it. Coming back in the dark we could easily have hit one of these rocks. Services like that were like looking for a needle in a haystack except that the haystack was the black sea and the needle was human life.

If the wind is from the south-east, east or north-east in Moelfre, when you go down the slipway, you are committed. The doors close behind you and you can't get back. Sometimes we were called out to the convoys to take off an injured man and we had to take the casualty round to Beaumaris. Well now, getting a sick man down from a big ship into a lifeboat bobbing up and down on its buoyancy tanks isn't easy. Imagine lowering down a man with a fractured spine. Sometimes the lifeboat would be several feet up the ship's side and the next moment way down in a trough. The casualty was lowered by stretcher and we had to unhook the sling. To get the hook out before the lifeboat dropped into the trough was very difficult work, especially when your hands were numb with cold.

When we did get him aboard we had to find our way to the Menai Strait. Not easy. There's a lighthouse at Penmon Point which is a guide to the Strait but it was very severely dimmed on account of the war. It was very, very difficult to find the narrow mouth of the Strait and, once we did get in, there are sandbanks on the port side and very nasty rocks on the starboard side. If you run too near the Caernarfon side you go aground; if you are too near the Anglesey side you get holed on the rocks. To try to navigate the lifeboat up that narrow channel, especially at low water, without any guiding light at all, with only the compass to help him, was a hard job for the cox'n.

Again, if the weather was bad we couldn't get into the cabin where the charts were stored because there was a possibility that when you opened the hatch to go down it would be flooded. The cox'n had to navigate out of his head. He had to know the courses everywhere around the vicinity of Moelfre. To Point Lynas, to the Isle of Man or to the Menai Strait. There were no lights, remember, and, of course, we had to go at full speed in case anything happened to the injured man. We had no wireless in the boat, no means of communication whatsoever. You couldn't even use the morse lamp. Sometimes we had as many as forty ships coming into Moelfre Bay. We had thirty-five minesweepers coming in every night and out the next morning to sweep the channel. They were very fast. Should one hit us when we were out they would simply go right through us. And they had very dim lights because they were just the craft the enemy planes would like to drop a bomb on. If you lived in Moelfre in those days the war at sea was your next-door-neighbour.

When Dick commanded the lifeboat himself, as he did on several occasions, he realized the magnitude of his uncle's task. 'I remember those times,' Dick continued, 'and think of what my Uncle John, the cox'n, did and I still can't believe we came out alive. His ability and his knowledge of the coast was remarkable.'

On 17 November 1943, in a 65mph gale five men were huddled in their inflatable dinghy, watching the tail of their aircraft sink below the waves. They could see waves breaking and paddled towards what they thought was the shore—but it was treacherous Dulas Island. When they reached it there was no foothold; all they could do was remain in the dinghy, cling to the jagged rocks and hope they would be seen.

The Moelfre lifeboat was already out searching for them. Hearing cries for help, the crew found the exhausted airmen, clutching the rocks, their hands raw and bloody. By the time the lifeboat came alongside—a difficult manoeuvre with engineer Robert Williams 'tickling' the engine to take the boat through the narrow race between the rocks—the airmen were semi-conscious.

Dick reached down from the bows of the lifeboat, but when he saw the dull eyes of the men in the dinghy, by now past caring what happened, he knew that they would be unable to help themselves. He is an immensely strong man and in that moment he thanked God for it. He would have to lean over, grab each man by the wrists and haul him—a dead weight in his soaking wet flying suit—into the lifeboat. The only asistance he would get would be from the sea itself. He waited for the next wave and, when it lifted the dinghy, he pulled out the first man. On the next rising wave, he grabbed another, until all five were safe. Finally he lifted the dinghy aboard.

The next morning the newspapers reported this superhuman effort by the 'Village Hercules'. Cox'n Matthews was subsequently awarded the RNLI silver medal for the rescue, and Dick and engineer Robert Williams each received bronze medals.

Once, with Dick in command, the Moelfre boat was called out to rescue the crew of a plane which had come down in the sea 25 miles north-west of Point Lynas. Though they searched for three hours in fog so thick it hid the bow of the lifeboat, they found no trace of it. Finally, out of the swirling mist, an air-sea rescue launch came on the scene. Greetings were exchanged. 'Since you're here,' Dick called across to the commander, 'there's little point in our staying. We might be needed somewhere else. We'd better be making for home, sir.'

The commander peered through the fog at the lifeboat below him, it looked tiny compared to his own craft, and had none of the launch's sophisticated gadgetry. 'How in God's name are you going to manage that?' he called back.

It was a fair question. The lifeboat was 25 miles out in a dense fog, but Dick had always had an instinct for finding his way home to a friendly port. Carefully estimating his course from their present position, taking speed and tides into consideration, they had been under way exactly three hours when Dick signalled for the engines to be cut. In the silence he heard surf breaking on rocks. They had reached the coast, but it would be madness to go any closer until daylight.

'Get the anchor ready,' he ordered. 'I'm not risking putting her ashore in this fog.'

He knew his crew, most of them well over sixty, hated the idea of spending the night at sea. But there were two bottles of rum, some biscuits and tins of corned beef in the locker; they would not starve. As he passed round the rum he thought he saw, over the stern, a flicker of light. There was only one young man in the crew. Dick called him over. 'I'm going ahead,' he said. 'I want you to go forward. The first sight or sound of breaking seas, holler your head off or we're on the rocks, for sure.'

The youngster scrambled into the bow. Gingerly, Dick moved forward at dead slow.

Years later he recalled the last moments: 'To my amazement we were at our slipway. It was pure luck. There were four ex-captains in the crew and when we got on the buoy I said, "Well, boys, what do you think of that for navigation?" '

' "Fantastic," they all said. "We could never have done it." Well, it was real luck.'

5

COXSWAIN

Dick's uncle, John Matthews, after thirty-six years as coxswain, decided in April 1954 that the time had come to swallow the anchor and hand over command of the lifeboat to his nephew. Dick had served a long apprenticeship: as a crew member from the age of sixteen, as bowman for eleven years and, since October 1939, as second coxswain. He now began seventeen and a half years as coxswain.

For Nansi, the life was perhaps more difficult than for the wives of other members of the crew. They had all been born into seafaring families, but she was a farmer's daughter. 'I'm not particularly interested in the sea,' she admitted. Nevertheless she did not try to deter Dick from taking on the full-time job which meant the fulfilment of his life's ambition. It would mean giving up his butcher's business and a drop in income; more than that, for Nansi there would be long hours of separation and a change in the pattern of their daily lives.

From now on, one or other of them must be within call by telephone every hour of the day or night. They could not even go to chapel together; one went in the morning, the other in the evening. It was Nansi's job to take down the instructions from the coastguards and, farmer's daughter or no, she never once made a mistake in the complicated messages.

While the lifeboat coxswain is a considerable figure in his community, he is, of necessity, a lonely man who must make difficult and sometimes life-and-death decisions concerning his friends and neighbours.

'It's not your own life,' Dick explains, 'it's your crew. When I thought I could do something spectacular and very risky I had to remember that I was risking other lives as well.'

Other responsibilities, while not so hazardous, were equally hard to carry out. A new RNLI regulation setting an age limit for lifeboatmen of sixty-five was to deprive Dick of most of his crew. When he had been a crew member himself, Dick had carried no responsibility beyond his own role in the boat. Now, signing off the older members, he felt for the first time the isolation of his command. It is hard to tell any man that he is too old to carry on. Some of them had been mature heroes when Dick was a boy and had continued their dedicated work of rescue right through the war.

He now had to form a stand-by crew of eight. Many men were away at sea or working outside the village, so this was a problem. Evan Owen, a crew member since the early days of the motor lifeboat, would stay on as engineer. Nor was there any difficulty in choosing a second coxswain: Murley Francis, a lifeboatman since boyhood, had been at sea for a number of years until he settled in the village with his wife and two small daughters. The baker, Maynard Davies, was appointed second mechanic. Alun Thomas, deputy surveyor for Anglesey County Council, had been in the Royal Navy during the war; a neighbour of Dick's, he was the obvious choice for bowman, but when first approached he was doubtful. 'I don't know anything about lifeboats, but if you think I'll be any use to you, Dick, I'd be honoured.'

Most lifeboatmen are qualified to practise first aid, but the recruitment of a doctor—William John Hughes, of Amlwch—extended their capabilities. 'We looked upon him as the Moelfre doctor,' Dick says. 'He was invaluable. Whenever I had a call that there was an injured man on a ship who needed to be taken ashore by the lifeboat—perhaps somebody had fallen down the engine-room ladder—I rang Dr Hughes. He never refused me. He had no experience of the sea; it was something that he was not used to, but he was always ready to volunteer. When you go on board a big liner you have to climb up these rope-ladders, which is very difficult. I used to climb up behind him carrying his bag. The funny thing was that he was never worried about himself, always the bag. I used to say, "Doctor, I'm right behind you," but he always replied, "Don't worry about me. For God's sake, don't drop the bag." '

Another neighbour, Will Jones, a baker's roundsman and wartime sailor, was taken on as emergency mechanic. More were needed to bring the crew up to the full complement; these came gradually. Well-paid jobs at the nearby Wylfa Nuclear Power Station lured young men away from seafaring and more recruits volunteered. Cousin Hugh Owen had been in the pull-and-sail boat which took part in the *Excel* rescue; a stone mason, he had left the village looking for work and on his return he signed on. Dick's crew was now complete.

Dick waited impatiently for his first call to service. At last he had been able to throw off his butcher's apron. There would be no more serving behind a counter, dancing attendance on housewives; no more bloody mornings in the slaughter-house. He was finished with cattle for ever—or so he thought.

> The first rescue I had [Dick recalls], was on a Saturday afternoon. I got a telephone call from a farmer William Innes that his cow had fallen over the cliffs near Point Lynas. Well, this had nothing at all to do with the lifeboat, a cow falling over the cliffs; but the farmer was demanding the lifeboat. I said, 'I can't launch. The lifeboat is to save lives.' He said, 'Well, hasn't a cow got life?'
>
> To make matters worse, the Hon Sec was away from the locality and I didn't know what to do. The farmer kept on at me. 'Are you going to let the cow drown?' I

said, 'What the dickens can I do? You want the RSPCA not the RNLI.'

No sooner had I got him off the phone than the RSPCA did come on and demanded me out, so I took the law into my own hands and I launched. I took a crew of three grammar-school boys and two old-age pensioners with me. We'd brought a punt we keep in the boat-house. The only possible way we could get near the cow was for two of the youngsters and one of the old boys—they were terrified of the cow—to go in the punt and put a rope round her neck.

There was about a hundred Anglesey farmers shouting on the cliffs telling us what to do. When they saw the rope going out they thought I was going to tow her on the end of a 100-fathom rope. I distinctly heard one say: 'The bloody fool is going to drown her.' He didn't realize I was trying to get the cow alongside the lifeboat. The poor animal was in a very bad way. She had been in the water for six hours, swimming. Sometimes she would get her front feet on a ledge, but she couldn't haul herself out. She was really struggling hard. We eventually managed to tie her alongside the boat and take her to a sandy beach. She walked away all right, but the amazing thing is what happened afterwards. The reason she could not scramble out of the water was that she was in calf. In two weeks' time that cow calved—after being in the water, remember, for six solid hours. And that same calf got the champion prize in the London Smithfield. The farmer proved to be a real gentleman. He gave the crew a good tip; and he told me to take my wife out to lunch and he gave me the price of a very substantial meal. I've thought since, what a wonderful advert it was for the RNLI to have rescued that little calf, which was at that time in the mother, that became champion at the Royal Smithfield.

That was my first rescue as cox'n, remember, and I still

had to face the Hon Sec, Colonel Williams. I'm proud to have known him. He was a grand gentleman, he really was, I thought the world of him. But I didn't know how to explain rescuing a cow.

I went up to his house on the Sunday and I wasn't keen on going. I was wondering if I'd done right. As soon as I was through the door he came forward. 'Splendid job, Evans,' he said. 'First rescue. You rescued a cow. We'll have to make a good report about this. But how are we going to describe it to the Institution in London? We can't say that you rescued a cow. Doesn't sound nice, somehow.'

'Could we say a heifer, sir?'

'Capital,' he said. 'We'll say a heifer though I doubt if they will know what a heifer is in London.'

Then he did something for sheer devilment. 'I want you to make a drawing,' he said. 'I want you to make a drawing of the heifer and how you rescued her. In case some cox'n ever has to do the same thing. It would be very beneficial to him.'

D'ye know, I was all night sketching. I only had to show the head and the horns and how to tie her alongside the lifeboat, but the cow looked more like a monkey. The amazing thing was that I got a letter from head office complimenting me on my drawing!

In 1956 the *George Ward*, having been launched seventy-one times and saving 147 lives on service calls, was taken out of service. She was replaced by the *Watkin Williams*, a 42ft, 12ft-beam, Watson-class boat, fitted with 48hp diesels and capable of a top speed of 8½ knots. Bought with a legacy from Miss Mary Eames Williams, of Deganwy, the new boat cost £27,800; today the price would be over £200,000. On 26 June 1956, Countess Howe named the boat which was destined to become part of the history of the sea.

A month later the *Watkin Williams* was called out on her first service. Red flares were seen and at 4.45am the lifeboat was launched into a bad sea and a north-easterly gale. She found the cabin cruiser *Leader* 5 miles east of Moelfre. The crew of three was rescued and their boat taken in tow.

As he put the *Watkin*'s helm back towards Moelfre, Dick was jubilant. Boats have personalities; some fractional difference in the building, some quirk of wood or stress of metal can alter the whole feel of a boat. The *Watkin* had proved herself, in difficult conditions, a superb craft. All boats are friends to Dick, but on this first rescue he felt a communion between himself and the *Watkin* which was to grow with every service. In time he would talk to her, implore, encourage and cajole her, reassuring her with soft words in frightening seas, urging her to an extra effort. Uncannily, the boat always seemed to respond.

The *Watkin* was much more sophisticated than her predecessors. The twin screws made her infinitely more manoeuvrable than the *GW* had been. She had a ship-to-shore radio and, for the first time, the crew could maintain reliable contact with the land. Now they could ask 'Charlie George', the Holyhead coastguard callsign, for up-to-the-minute weather reports and information about the position of ships in distress.

To the lifeboatmen's families, 'Charlie George' took on human form and was looked on as a guardian, in the way the coastguards themselves were to the crews. One night when Dick was out on a service, his wife and three sons sat by the fire, waiting. 'I wonder where they are,' said Nansi. 'It's a very rough night.'

'Don't worry, mum!' said Derek, the youngest, 'Mr Charlie George will look after him.'

In the earlier boats, soundings were taken with a 12lb lead line knotted at intervals to indicate the fathom mark. The *Watkin Williams* had an echo-sounder. For the first time,

(above)
The heroes of the *Nafsiporos* aboard the lifeboat at Moelfre (*Liverpool Daily Post & Echo*)

(below)
Dick Evans with his three sons. From left to right: David, Dick, William and Derek (*Liverpool Daily Post & Echo*)

(above)
John Mathews, Dick's uncle who was coxswain of the Moelfre lifeboat for thirty-six years before Dick took his place (*Liverpool Daily Post & Echo*)

(below)
Dick Evans and Lt. Commander Harold Harvey in London to receive the Gold Medals they won on the *Nafsiporos* rescue (*RNLI*)

the crew knew exactly when they were near the sandbanks and could change course into deeper water.

Dick not only had a good boat but a superb crew. 'The younger men were just what I needed,' he recalls. 'The old boys would never have understood the new improvements. It's especially important to have a reliable winchman and three good men on the slipway to help him. They get the boat launched but, more important, they help to get it back, which is very tricky. You have to fit a 10in keel into a 12in keelway and get the bridle rope on the stern before you can fix the hauling-up wire—not easy in a rough sea.

'What I used to do if there was a member of my regular crew short, I'd choose the best man on the slipway to come into the boat. He would know a little about the lifeboat having helped on the slipway and gradually these men became regular members of the crew. Murley Francis, the second cox, had been on the slipway as a very young boy, so had Hugh Owen.

'I had a very good crew and I respected and trusted them. They were splendid boys. On many a wild night when we came ashore wet to the skin, half frozen, very hungry and very miserable at times, I've said to myself, "I don't suppose I'll see these fellows again." And I couldn't have blamed them either. But a few days later there would be another service and there would be the same faces looking up at me from under the canopy, ready for anything.'

Ironically, when the testing time came for Dick, it was not at sea but on land. The stomach pain had been with him for years. He had to give up his favourite dishes; he could no longer eat bacon, and meat pies made him ill. He lived on milk puddings until he could not bear to see a cow grazing in a field. He began to lose weight. One day on the beach an old shipmate said bluntly, 'You are dying on your feet.'

At last Dick agreed to go to Liverpool Royal Infirmary for

a check-up. An X-ray showed that the duodenum was blocked and an immediate operation necessary. For a man who had never been ill in his life going into hospital was a traumatic experience. By now he was convinced he had cancer; the disease had killed his mother and he had gone through every spasm of her pain as he watched by her bed. Certain that he was going to die, and loathing the malignant thing he believed was growing inside him, he became deeply depressed.

He knew about seas and boats, winds and tides, but in the Infirmary he was like a wild bird, caged. Outwardly stoical—he had learned how to control fear and cover it with a placid face—his heart was thudding against his ribs as he was prepared for the operation.

He explains:

> None of us wants to die. We talk about the everlasting life and the wonderful heaven we are going to, but we want to stay in this old world. Under the anaesthetic I dreamed I was going across the Mersey on a ship. When I awoke I had been moved to another part of the hospital. I didn't recognize my surroundings. I came to believe the trip across the Mersey was not a dream. I had been taken out of the Infirmary. I had cancer and I was going to die. It was no use the nurses trying to persuade me I was still in the Infirmary. I was, of course, but I would not believe it. I even made a little speech thanking them for their kindness, but explained, 'I knew before I came here I was a dying man. There is nothing you can do.'

The tremendous inner strength, which had sustained him during the *Hindlea* rescue, unaccountably deserted him. He convinced himself he was not going to get well—more than that, he stopped trying to get well.

In the end another dream brought Dick back to life. He

recalls it vividly: 'I was on a wheel, trying to get over but I couldn't. Then I saw my grandmother with a little shawl over her shoulders. She was helping me over.'

There was a minister of religion in the bed next to Dick. When he recounted the dream, the minister said, 'I've often thought it would be difficult for God to be everywhere; there are so many calls. What more natural than that he should have agents? And who better to see you through the crisis of your operation than the grandmother you loved?'

To Dick, a man of uncomplicated beliefs and loyalty to old-fashioned family codes, this point of view was unassailable. An unexpected visit from a stranger, a retired sea captain who had sailed with his father, gave him further proof that his family were watching and caring.

'I don't know what made me come,' his visitor admitted. 'But when I heard you were ill it suddenly came on me that your father would have liked me to visit you. You must get well and get back to the wonderful work you are doing in the lifeboat.'

Thanks to the doctors at the Liverpool Royal Infirmary, and the nurses whom Dick still thinks of as 'angels', it was not long before he was back with the *Watkin Williams*.

A lifeboat coxswain is on twenty-four hour call all his working life. Inevitably, since he spends more time at the station than in his own home, his leisure activities are confined to the things he can do in a boat or on the seashore. In Moelfre and a thousand other villages like it this meant fishing.

'I don't know whether we were poaching or not,' Dick explains. 'We were catching salmon in the open sea. I can't for the life of me understand why this was ever made illegal. I can understand the rivers, that you have to have a licence in the rivers. But, surely, in the open sea it doesn't do any harm to anybody?

'This was a happy time and we enjoyed it. We were working for a very small salary for the lifeboats. The fishing was pocket money to buy baccy. We used to take another old captain, Tom Idwal Jones, with us. He could smell a salmon miles off. He never did any work. The mechanic and me did all the work and he was bossing all the time. But there's no doubt about it, he was brilliant. He knew exactly where the salmon were. He's been dead many years now and I miss him a lot.

'Fishing for salmon in the open sea had been done in Moelfre for hundreds of years. It's totally disallowed now, but in those days we didn't know we were doing wrong, we enjoyed it. We put an anchor down on the sand—we had to to do it on a sandy beach or the net would catch in the rocks—and then we rowed out, paying the net out as we went. When we came ashore at the other end of the beach the net would be in the shape of a horseshoe. One man would run to the far end and, gradually narrowing the horseshoe, we pulled the net in. It was very hard work, but it was very exciting indeed when we could see the salmon flapping in the nets. Very exciting.

'The mechanic and I were not allowed to leave the village. We always had to be within call. I remember very well one night we were dragging for salmon. We were having a very good catch when we heard a terrible bang. We left the net and everything on the sand and drove the boat as hard as we could. We thought this bang was a maroon, calling out the lifeboat, and we were really terribly upset, both of us, because there would be nobody there to take the boat out. But when we approached the boat-house there was no sign of anybody. It turned out it had been a plane breaking the sound barrier.

'Another night the mechanic phoned me and asked me would I consider going out fishing that night. I don't know why, it was a lovely evening, but I thought, "No, I'm not feeling too good," so we didn't go. There were four boats out that night. The first boat came in and as they were landing in the bay the beach was suddenly all lit up with car headlights. The skipper said, "My God, these English visitors are very good, you know. They've put the lights on their cars for us to see to bring the nets up."

'Two or three of these "gentlemen" went down to the boat and asked the skipper, "Did you have a good catch?"

' "*Duw*," he said, "a very good catch. And thank you for shining the light."

'They were so friendly that he showed them the net and the catch, and they helped him carry them up the beach. It was only when they got to the top that they disclosed they were Board of Fisheries inspectors, and they confiscated both nets and fish.

'Now there were three other boats out and there was no chance for anyone to warn them. The second boat came in and the same thing happened to them. Nets and fish were confiscated. The third boat came in. The same.

'Now the fourth boat landed on another little beach by Moelfre Island. The owner was an ex-captain, and a very nice gentleman. He went out purely for the fun of it and for a feed of salmon; he never sold them.

'The fishery officials couldn't understand what had happened when his engine stopped. Someone said, "Oh, he's having another trawl." The others knew very well he had landed and they wanted to give him a chance to get away.

'I met Tom later on and he said, "Were you out last night?" "No," I said, "I wasn't." "Well," he said, "they'll have to use a very fine comb to find my nets." It turned out he'd taken them about four miles away and hidden them at a farm.'

On 28 July 1957 Dick was presented with one of the most difficult decisions of his career. He describes what happened that day:

It was Sunday afternoon and we were called out with the lifeboat. It was blowing very hard and a girl swimmer was being carried out to sea. There is a freshwater river in Red Wharf Bay with dangerous currents in its channel. This girl was caught in one and she couldn't get back. There was a heavy sea and it took us three-quarters of an hour to get to her. When I reached her I saw two more heads in the water. Two men had gone out in a small boat to rescue her and it had capsized. The boat was only about 8ft long and low in the water. When it turned over it wouldn't hold the weight of the two men.

The cox'n of a lifeboat has some nasty, cruel decisions to make at times. This was one of them. I was duty bound to save the girl first, but I knew that those two men would have drowned if I had gone to the girl. Now, I had my son David with me and he's a very good swimmer. I asked him did he think if he dived over and swam to this girl he could keep afloat. He said, 'Yes.'

It wasn't easy for me to send my own son over the side—we were going full speed, you know—but he knew exactly what to do. He was highly trained in life-saving. I had told him: 'When you reach the girl and you have got her safely, raise one arm up perpendicular.' I told one of the members of the crew, 'Now, watch David. Tell me exactly what's happening. Don't take your eyes off David.'

You can imagine my feeling. Trying to rescue those men and thinking maybe I have sent my own son to his death. And this man who was watching David, he said: 'Oh my God, cox'n, there's something wrong with David. He's raising his hand straight up.'

'Thank God,' I said, 'I know he's all right now.' The two

men were in a very bad way. They were really exhausted. We got them on board and put the boat about. We had to approach the girl very, very slowly because when a person has been in the water for two or three hours they vanish in the twinkling of an eye almost. And David was on his back with this girl on his chest, just playing about with one hand in the water. He shouted, 'Just take your time, dad, I'm all right.' We got her into the boat and she too was in a very bad way, believe me. I've never seen a person alive in the state that girl was in. Her eyes were wide open and her heart was thumping as if a machine was driving it. You could hear it thumping over the engines. One of these men that we'd rescued came out from the canopy with a blanket round him and he said, 'For God's sake, cox'n, give her some rum.'

This was against the regulations of first aid. I knew you shouldn't give anything intoxicating to a person that was apparently drowned. It was dead against the rules. But he got hold of my wrist and he squeezed it, 'For God's sake, give her rum or she'll die.' It was only then that I realized he was the village doctor, but I was still dubious—was he losing control of himself? Very hesitant I got the rum bottle out—was I doing the right thing? He asked me, 'How long will it take you to get back?' 'At least half an hour.' 'Too late,' he said. 'I only give her ten minutes to live.' What the doctor wanted was to get her into a hot bath. The only thing I could do was to drive the lifeboat onshore. Now it was a brand new boat. It was only a year since we'd brought the *Watkin Williams* to Moelfre. I didn't know the vicinity well, I could be driving her on to rocks. I could see a jeep driving down the beach at Benllech and I thought, if I could beach the boat on the sand, the crew could carry the girl ashore. When we hit the sand I could hear it soughing under the keel. It was a nasty moment. The crew ran up the beach, put the girl and the doctor into the jeep and it went off to the nearest house.

Somebody telephoned Colonel Williams and told him the lifeboat was high and dry on Benllech sands. I was hiding when he came down. I was ashamed of the lifeboat being high and dry with thousands of visitors all around looking at it, but I need not have worried. It would not have mattered if I had run that lifeboat on to rocks, possibly causing damage costing thousands of pounds, provided we saved life. One life. This is what makes the RNLI such a wonderful organization. It's lifesaving that's their only concern. The committee of management in London, they do everything with that in mind. I know, after forty-nine years with the RNLI, that they do everything possible to save life.

6

THE NEW INSHORE LIFEBOAT

During Dick's time as coxswain, a significant change took place in the pattern of the lifeboat service. The boom in the demand for small boats in the affluent 1960s meant that, throughout the summer months, holidaymakers around the coasts of Britain were putting to sea in a variety of pleasure craft. All too often they got into difficulties—outboard motors broke down, sailing dinghies capsized, inflatable mattresses were swept away by wind and current. In such emergency situations, where speedy action and manoeuvrability were called for, the conventional lifeboat was too slow both in launching and in pursuit. A small boat, reported in trouble 2 miles from shore, might drift a further 3 miles before the rescue crew was under way. An inflated raft, carrying a child, could be blown by the wind at a speed beyond the reach of the big lifeboat. A different kind of rescue craft was needed and, to supplement the work of the larger vessels, the RNLI started to build up a fleet of inflatable inshore lifeboats.

Moelfre received its first ILB in 1965. Initially, Dick was unimpressed. It lacked style, it was just a flat-iron shaped inflated tube not unlike a tractor tyre; and its two-man crew found it extremely uncomfortable, particular in rough weather. But its 60hp engine gave it a fine turn of speed—it was 12 knots faster than the 8½-knot *Watkin Williams.* Not only could it be launched in a matter of seconds, but it had another advantage. The big lifeboat is unable to get back to the Moelfre station against winds from the east, south or north-east, while the inshore boat can be brought right up on to the beach. It was not long before Dick became one of the ILB's most ardent supporters—although, when he talked of 'his boat', everyone took it for granted he was referring to the *Watkin Williams*.

No one clings to tradition with more fervour than an old seadog, but Dick now believes the ILBs are the best thing to have happened to the RNLI. 'I've had experience of going out and snatching children, on the verge of drowning, off sandbanks that the bigger boats could not have got near.'

The Moelfre ILB's first effective service was on 1 August 1965. She was launched at 1.25pm within five minutes of the first sighting of a disabled motor boat, the *Maddick*, drifting out to sea, and rescued the crew of three. The same afternoon the ILB went to the aid of another motor boat, the *Seacrest*, in difficulties in a choppy sea. The following day, she was called out to a rowing boat sinking fast 5 miles east-south-east of the boat-house, and took off five people. Four days later six people were rescued when another rowing boat was being blown out to sea.

Averaging fifty service calls a year, the ILBs are out more often than the traditional lifeboats. On 20 August 1968 the Moelfre ILB was called out on four separate services. The first was to escort a sailing dinghy to safety; and the second, at 5.30pm, was to a small motor boat drifting out in choppy seas before a south-westerly wind, when two adults and three children were rescued. The ILB returned to her station at 6.25pm and, twenty-five minutes later, went to the aid of a sailing dinghy that had capsized 2½ miles south of the boat-house. Two men, clinging to the capsized boat, were pulled on board the ILB and, with the dinghy lashed to the side, taken to Traeth Bychan. On the way back to Moelfre, the inshore lifeboat's crew came upon a canoeist trying without success to make headway against the wind and tide. The man and his canoe were hauled aboard and landed at

Benllech. The ILB returned to Moelfre at 8pm and, three minutes later, the crew were called out again to a small boat reported in difficulties 2 miles south of the boat-house. The two men on board were rescued and their boat towed to Traeth Bychan. At 8.30pm the ILB was back in the station at Moelfre.

'The saddest rescue in which I was involved affected me very deeply,' Dick recalls. 'Lifeboatmen are looked upon as hard, tough men, but every one of us has a soft heart or we wouldn't be in the job. Most of us are fathers and when something happened as it did on this particular day it really cuts our hearts to ribbons.

'I was in the boat-house with the mechanic Evan Owen. Our two sons, both called David, were with us. It was a nice evening, the tide was up nearly to high water. The telephone rang and we were told that a boat had sunk at Porth-yr-Aber, barely half a mile from our slipway. The two Davids, being young men, got the inshore lifeboat out and, from the time the telephone rang, they were on the spot in two minutes. There was a doctor, Percy Whittaker, a radiologist, in a small boat. In the bows sat a holidaymaker, John Dunhill, with his ten-year-old daughter, Jennifer, in his arms. As the inshore lifeboat went alongside, Mr Dunhill was shouting: "My little girl, Carol, is down there," and he was pointing into the sea. My son David dived in and, 20ft below found the sunken boat, perpendicular. Of course, the weight of the outboard engine would do that. He swam round the boat and looked inside, but he could see no sign of anyone. He came up to the surface again and the man shouted: "Her hair is caught in the flywheel of the engine."

'David swam down again, hooked his feet under the thwart of the boat and struck out for the surface, pulling the boat after him. He came up close to the ILB and David

Owen was able to grab the boat. He was frantic himself by this time; my David had been down for a long time and David Owen had seen a stream of bubbles coming up. Between them they managed to haul the boat into the ILB and there was the little darling, she was only seven, hanging by her hair from the engine. The doctor, now, had come alongside. He cut the little girl's hair, lifted her into the boat and all the way back to the slipway he gave her artificial respiration. A helicopter arrived and hovered over the ILB until it got to the slipway. The little child was carried up and laid on a bench in the boat-house.

'Dr Whittaker, the pilot of the helicopter and myself took it in turns to give the girl artificial respiration. We worked on that little girl for nearly two hours but eventually the doctor said she was dead.

'I was very cut up indeed. I had a little granddaughter of my own. It really upset me and I'm not ashamed of saying that I wept for hours. To make matters worse, her grandfather forced his way past the police who had been keeping the crowds away from the boat-house. I shall never forget him. He said, "My darling little babby," and he put his arms round her and kissed her and hugged her. Oh, my God, it was terrible. That's the most heart-breaking thing that happened to me since I've been in the lifeboat service. Everything humanly possible was done to save that little girl's life but to no avail.'

For his part in the rescue attempt David Evans was awarded the Royal Humane Society bronze medal. David's swimming feats are legendary. Once, while serving at sea, he dived 25ft from the bridge of a tanker into the Firth of Forth to save a dinghy sailor from drowning. A few months later, on the same ship in dock at Grangemouth, David again dived to the rescue of one of the crew who had fallen overboard. An account of this incident, for which he also received the Royal Humane Society's medal, appeared in the local paper. The man David had rescued earlier from the Firth of Forth read the report and contacted the press. His first exploit, rather belatedly, came to the attention of his employers and the shipping line presented him with a gold watch.

All three of Dick's sons inherited their father's passion for the sea and have in turn served in the lifeboat. Derek, a police sergeant, holds a Royal Humane Society's citation for diving, in full uniform, from the harbour wall at Caernarfon to save a drowning man.

William, his other son, was with Dick when both of them got into difficulties, as he remembers:

'Lifeboat Day is a very important occasion in Moelfre. We launch the boat and give a demonstration of lifesaving. It's in the summer when the visitors are here and thousands of people come down to the station. We have a helicopter to demonstrate how it assists the lifeboat in rescues at sea. It is a day we train for quite a lot, the big event of the year.

'The day before Flag Day, I had been painting one of my little boats. I couldn't leave the station, of course, so I painted it on the slip. We had a dozen lobster pots down. My son William came down and we launched the little punt down the slipway in the same way we launched the lifeboat. The next thing I knew the punt had capsized and I was in the water. I had oilskin trousers on and a pair of sea boots and, don't forget, I was getting on. We were quite a way out and my son was swimming round me shouting, "Are you all right, dad?"

' "I'm all right. You make for the slipway, I'll reach it."

'A retired sea captain had been watching us from the cliffs. This old chap said, apparently, "Oh my God, I'm looking at two men drowning. And I can't do nothing to help them." It must have been looking very bad to him with the boat turning over 40 yards out in a choppy sea. All the timber floating out of it, the oars and everything and us two struggling in the water. Do you know, when I reached the slipway I was really exhausted, but when I scrambled out on to the slip I still had my pipe in my mouth!'

Sometimes the two Moelfre lifeboats worked in tandem and, on one occasion at least, they were joined by a helicopter. The inshore boat went out first to pick up three men stranded off Llanddona after their power boat broke down. Seconds after landing them, the ILB was out again, chasing a sailing dinghy with four men aboard being blown out to sea in a squall. They were followed by the *Watkin Williams* which was called out to aid another dinghy, that had lost its mast off Moelfre Island. On the same service the lifeboat stood by while a helicopter from RAF Valley winched up a weekend sailor whose boat had capsized. Eleven people were rescued by these combined efforts.

An apparently uncomplicated rescue could turn into a life-and-death struggle. On one occasion a 50ft barge—a converted RAF launch—had been anchored in Benllech Bay while divers carried out an underwater survey for a new sewerage scheme. A force 6 on-shore wind suddenly blew up and the divers' jolly-boat was instantly carried away. Only one engine on the barge was functioning and she began to drag her anchor. Huge breakers were building up between the barge and the shore. The survey team, all experienced divers, realized it was too risky to try to swim ashore. Yet they were not much safer on the barge which was being pulled towards the breakers.

When the news of the men's plight reached Moelfre Station, Dick knew he had to act fast. He had been working on the *Watkin Williams* with his nineteen-year-old son, William—then awaiting a place at University College, Cardiff. In the engine-room were Evan Owen and his son David, aged twenty-seven and an electrical engineer with

Cunard. Outside the station, Dick found Goronwy Williams, a council tractor driver, and his pal Will Rowlands, a seaman on leave from the Merchant Navy. Apart from Evan Owen—a veteran of the *Hindlea* rescue the year before—Dick's hastily assembled crew were young and comparatively untried.

The *Watkin* was launched into a 60mph gale in torrential rain. The bow buried itself in the surf and Dick braced himself behind the wheel as the sea broke over him, seeping through every gap in his oilskins, soaking him to the skin. Evan gunned the engine and, with twin screws screaming, they were under way at maximum revs.

Benllech Bay is one of the most crowded beaches on the island, but the holidaymakers who paddle and play in its tranquil waters would hardly have recognized it that day as angry waves crashed against the rocks, creating whirlpools of milky spray. Daggers of rain, blown horizontally by the gale, ripped blindingly into Dick's face.

The survey barge was right in amongst the breakers, taking a terrible pounding. Diving gear, galley utensils and cables were sliding about her deck; broken spars and pieces of equipment swirled in the water. To the men on board, the sight of the lifeboat must have seemed like salvation, but it was too shallow for Dick to bring her alongside nor could he use the breeches buoy. In that sea not even the lifeboat could hold her own; she was being dragged inshore by the breaking sea and Dick could feel the sand pulling at the keel. Five times Dick pushed the *Watkin* into the turmoil of surf and five times she was blown back through the treacherous shallows. So slight seemed the chance of success that Dick radioed to RAF Valley for a helicopter. Replacing the hand microphone, he determined to make one last attempt. As the *Watkin* approached, the barge's anchor chain snapped and the main cable shot out of the water, flailing wildly, over Dick's head to crash back into the sea astern.

Finally, they came near enough to the barge for two of her crew to jump into the lifeboat. But she was carried away again, leaving the other three still slithering on the barge's treacherous decks. It took several more dangerous runs before all the survey men were safely off and the *Watkin* was able to fight her way out of the shallows into deeper water. She was badly damaged. One of her crew leaned over the side and the news he signalled back to the wheel was alarming. In the buffeting she had received in the shallows, the lifeboat's bow had been holed. There was no question of returning to Moelfre in the seas she was encountering. Dick would have to take her round the Penmon rocks and up the narrow channel of the Strait to Beaumaris.

In the Strait the graph on the echo-sounder drew a frightening picture of cliffs and valleys as the crippled lifeboat was pushed to the edge of sandbanks which had wrecked much bigger vessels. At last they saw the outline of Beaumaris pier, but the lifeboat was too severely damaged to be tied up at the landing stage. She had to be moored off the slipway and the men taken ashore by dinghy.

A relief service had already been organized. Dry clothing had been rushed by car from Moelfre, and the Beaumaris coxswain, Hugh Jones, Alderman Mary Burton and a lifeboat supporter, Joe Clayton, were waiting on the landing stage with food and hot drinks. Three and a half hours had passed since the *Watkin* was launched in Moelfre.

The RAF helicopter had reached the scene just as the survey team were rescued. 'Sandy' Davidson, the pilot said later: 'Visibility was poor; there was driving rain and the sea was very, very rough. I don't know how the lifeboat did it.'

Dick's own comment was short and to the point: 'It was nearly as bad as the *Hindlea*.'

I've been asked on several occasions what did I get out

(above)
The crew of the *Watkin Williams*, left to right: Evan Owen (mechanic), Hugh Jones, David Evans (Dick's eldest son), Dick Evans, Hugh Owen, Donald Murley Francis (second cox), Maynard Davies (assistant mechanic). Captain Jeavons, one of the crewmen in the *Nafsiporos* rescue, was away at sea commanding the *Empress of Canada* (*RNLI*)

(below)
From left to right: Dick Evans, Evan Owen, Donald Murley Francis, Hugh Owen and Hugh Jones outside Buckingham Palace after the Queen had presented them with their silver medals for gallantry at sea in the rescue of the *Hindlea* (*RNLI*)

(above)
Dick Evans receives his RNLI Gold Medal from Princess Marina, Duchess of Kent, which he was awarded for his outstanding courage in the rescue of *Hindlea*'s crew (*Liverpool Daily Post & Echo*)

(below)
Dick with his wife Nansi at Buckingham Palace after receiving the BEM (*Liverpool Daily Post & Echo*)

of risking my life the way I have. I've had no financial benefit at all out of it, but I have had tremendous satisfaction. You just think, now [Dick said in a rare moment of self-revelation] I have gone out on several occasions in the ILB and plucked a drowning man out of the water. The wonderful gratitude in that man's eyes . . . or when I have picked up a little child from a sandbank—just about to be submerged—and carried it back and delivered it safely into its mother's arms. The sincere 'thank you', the gratitude in the face of the mother has compensated me for all the hardship I have had.

It's only when it's all over, when you're sitting in your home in your own armchair, you go over these things. Do you know, sometimes I get terribly frightened, whereas in the lifeboat I wasn't; I was too occupied. I'm sitting going over things and sometimes I'm leaping out of the chair. These things come vividly to your mind. Indeed, after I've been out on a rescue, my wife doesn't get a wink of sleep with me. I'm leaping in bed, I'm screaming sometimes when I think I'm seeing a tremendous snarling wave coming towards the boat, threatening to swallow us for ever. And these things tell on you, you know. And yet, I must say, I enjoyed it all. I would do the same thing over again.

7

THE RESCUE OF THE *NAFSIPOROS*

When the 1,287-ton Greek freighter ss *Nafsiporos* had unloaded her cargo at Liverpool on 29 November 1966, there was very little ballast in her holds. On the return passage to Belfast she was in peril from the moment she crossed the Mersey Bar and hit the cyclone. Light as she was, the seas she encountered harried her at will, and her screws were lifted clean out of the water. The crew of nineteen had to struggle to keep their footing on the pitching deck.

On the bridge, the twenty-nine-year-old chief mate, Evangelos Pittas, reported to the skipper, Angelo Katsovufis, 'We can't steer. Whenever the screws come out of the water we lose control. And they're out most of the time.'

Katsovufis, a twenty-eight-year-old bachelor, received the information silently, weighing the chances. *Nafsiporos* was his first command; he had held it for only a month and could not afford to make a wrong decision now. No cargo skipper likes to lose time on passage, but the lives of his men were at stake. Katsovufis went over to the chart table. The nearest land was the Isle of Man; if he could reach it, the cliffs would offer some shelter from the worst of the weather. 'Set a course for Ramsey,' he ordered. 'We'll anchor there and ride it out.'

The passage was difficult and it was the evening of the 30th before they came under the lee of the Manx headland. Even there the seas were in turmoil and the roar of the wind drowned the rattle of the chain as the anchor was paid out. At last it struck and *Nafsiporos* lurched as its tynes bit into the sea bottom.

'There's nothing more we can do now except pray that the anchor holds,' Katsovufis told the mate. 'I'm going below. Call me at once if our situation changes.'

The off-duty watch lay in their bunks. They were wet, hungry and miserable. The galley fire had been doused and none of the men had eaten hot food since they embarked. The rum they had drunk to combat the cold churned in their empty guts, sending waves of nausea into their throats. None of them could sleep as they listened to the bulkhead plates straining against the force of the sea and the crash of the anchor chain on the steel deck above them. They knew their lives depended on the strength of the chain; if it snapped they would be wholly at the mercy of the sea. Their bodies gradually settled to the rocking rhythm of the boat, as she rode each succeeding swell of water. If it was like this in the shelter of the land, they wondered, what would it be like in the open sea?

First light on 2 December was watery and hesitant. The watches were changing when the bosun, Angelo Mougis, felt an ominous shift in the motion of the ship. 'We're moving,' he cried. 'We're moving.'

In his cabin, the young skipper had been lying fully dressed on his bunk.

'She's dragging her anchor, sir,' the chief mate told him. 'We're going to lose it.'

'Let's get up to the bridge,' the captain replied, 'and see what we can do.'

There was nothing to be done. The engines were useless against the pull of the sea. Like a plastic toy, *Nafsiporos* was being driven crabwise before the wind. Once again the crew heard the scream of the screws as the ship reared up out of the water.

The skipper and his mate were joined on the bridge by chief engineer John Patsoulas, at thirty-eight the oldest man aboard. 'I don't know how long we can last,' he reported. 'The engines are overheating like crazy. It's only a matter of time before they break down.'

Driven by winds gusting at 100 knots and with her engines failing, *Nafsiporos* was plunging wildly and uncontrollably in beam seas. The radio operator was sending out frantic May Day calls, when, with a shudder, the engines stopped.

Nafsiporos had been reported in distress 12 miles south of Douglas Bay. The rescue operation had begun at 8.20pm. The wind was already reaching 90 knots and the seas were, according to the official report, 'exceptionally heavy'.

The Douglas lifeboat—the 46ft 9in Watson-class *R. A. Colby Cobbin No 1*—was launched, with Cox'n Robert Lee at the wheel. With visibility down to 500 yards and spindrift as thick as fog, he could find no trace of the crippled vessel. Then, at 10.06am, came a report that she had been sighted at 9.50am by the Ramsey coastguard; she was now 23½ miles from Douglas Head. An hour later another sighting was radioed. A Coastal Command Shackleton from RAF Kinloss had now joined the search and was circling the freighter 25 miles from the Head.

By 11.52 coastguards estimated the lifeboat to be within 5½ miles of the Greek ship. A few minutes afterwards Cox'n Lee sighted the Shackleton and altered course towards it. Half an hour later he established radio contact with the aircraft, but owing to poor visibility the Shackleton was unable to direct the lifeboat to the freighter. The *Colby Cobbin* continued her search until 6.30pm when, her fuel running low, she had to return to her station.

Nafsiporos, totally helpless by now, was meanwhile being driven nearer and nearer to the notoriously dangerous Skerries, off the northern coast of Anglesey.

That morning Lieut-Commander Harold Harvey, the

RNLI Inspector of Lifeboats for the North-West, was motoring through Holyhead on his way to a meeting at Trearddur Bay. He decided to pay a courtesy call on the Holyhead lifeboat secretary, Tudor Roberts. A new coxswain, Tom Alcock, a former bowman on the Rhyl lifeboat, had that year been appointed to Holyhead and Commander Harvey wanted to check on the arrangements to provide him with a house. Arriving at Tudor Roberts' home at 10.15, he was told that *Nafsiporos* had been sighted 20 miles north of Point Lynas, drifting fast towards the rocks. Roberts, who had been unable to telephone the lifeboat station as all the lines were down, had just left for the boat-house to order the launching of the lifeboat. Commander Harvey followed him down.

There was consternation at the boat-house. With the telephone out of order and the sound of the maroons, which had been fired at 10.12, lost in the wind, there was no way of summoning the crew. Commander Harvey immediately volunteered as an extra hand.

The Holyhead lifeboat—the 52ft Barnett-type *St Cybi*—was launched at 10.30. Ten minutes later—two hours before high water—she passed the breakwater and hit the open sea. A north-westerly force 10 gale, gusting to force 11, was already lashing the sea into a frenzy. After searching for three hours in these appalling conditions, the crew sighted a Shackleton 2 miles to the east, at 1.30pm. The aircraft's crew was now able to see the lifeboat and direct her on an easterly course. At 1.38, the *St Cybi* made contact with *Nafsiporos*.

The Russian timber ship, *Kungurley*, had picked up the freighter's May Day signals and changed course to go to her aid. She arrived on the scene ahead of a number of other ships which had also joined the search. After many attempts the Russians managed to get a line aboard the freighter. She was yawing 60 degrees to both port and starboard; many of her crew, tossed about like toffee in a box, sustained minor injuries and all were violently seasick. Somehow they made fast the tow—a feat in itself in those seas—and waited for the Russians to take up the slack. At first it seemed that all was well and the two ships made some progress. But after twenty-five minutes it proved impossible to get *Nafsiporos* head to sea. A beam wave struck her, the tow tightened, the heavy wire cable snapped like garden twine and once again the freighter was adrift. There was not enough sea-room for the Russians to reconnect the tow, but *Kungurley* was still standing by when the Holyhead lifeboat arrived.

The Moelfre lifeboat had been called out at 7.40am to the aid of the MV *Vinland*, reported to have developed engine trouble. It took the *Watkin Williams* two and a half hours to reach her position 5 miles north of Point Lynas, scarcely 7 sea miles from their station. A radio-telephone message from the coastguard then reported that the steering gear of a second motor vessel, the *Grit*, had broken down and she was in trouble 3½ miles north-east of the *Watkin*. The coastguard left Dick to decide which vessel to aid. The *Grit* had much less sea-room and was nearer his present position, but it took another three hours to reach her. They stood by until the motor vessel radioed that the steering gear had been repaired and help was no longer needed. Meanwhile another ship, *Pacific North West*, had found the *Vinland*, and the tug, *Utrecht*, radioed that she was on her way to give assistance.

Gratefully, Dick put about to return to Moelfre. He remembers:

> The passage was very rough, but as we were running before the sea with a drogue out, the *Watkin* handled splendidly. We reached Moelfre and made fast the hauling rope. We were halfway up the slip when my winchman, Richard Lewis ran down. 'There's an urgent message from Holyhead coastguard,' he shouted.

I went to the telephone and the coastguard told me to launch again. We were wanted to help the Holyhead boat with the *Nafsiporos*. My crew were very cold, tired and hungry, but nobody argued when I told them we had to go out again. We refuelled and at 1.55pm we launched for the second time that day.

The tide was ebbing by this time, running against the wind. I daren't open the chart room in case the sea flooded in. A cox on those old lifeboats couldn't look at charts; he had to carry them in his head. I knew the rocks, the set and drift of tides, the currents. But that day the sea was like a foreign country. With the leaping and plunging of the lifeboat, the compass was swinging wildly. I could see nothing. The sea was being blown into clouds of spray and visibility was nil. We had to run on dead reckoning. The lifeboat was travelling at 8 knots which meant that we should come up with the Holyhead boat within three hours allowing for the need to reduce speed. I set a course well outside Point Lynas, 5½ miles away, although we would still pass Dulas Island and its rocks.

The waves were like nothing I'd ever been told about. We climbed perpendicularly and we went down the same way. I was afraid every wave was going to send us somersaulting on our back. There would have been no hope for any of us then, we would have disappeared for ever.

The Holyhead coastguard warned us over the radio that the wind, which was on our starboard bow, was gusting at 120mph. It was something you read of in sea tales. A 60mph wind is terrible, but a 120mph gale hardly ever happened. Tremendous waves were washing over the lifeboat, but she behaved magnificently and at least the seas were breaking on our bows. A beam sea would have finished us.

I did not see Point Lynas and I had to guess where we were to set the 11-mile course to the Skerries rocks. We crashed on through terrible waves like mountains. As the lifeboat climbed up she was almost vertical. My worry was what we were going to meet on the other side. I was out of my own patrol area by this time and I did not know these seas at all. We were all frozen; we had been soaked, as we always were, by the launching and I asked Murley to go below and get out the rum. Nobody drinks lifeboat rum because they like it—it burns the skin off the inside of your cheeks. But my legs were getting weak and I needed a reviver. I put the lifeboat dead slow, head on to wind, and I called to Murley down the speaking-tube that it was safe to come back. 'I'm very sorry, Dick,' he said. 'The bottle's smashed. It jumped out of my hand.' I told him to put the second bottle inside his life-jacket, I thought it would be safe in there, but the boat took a terrific leap and unshipped the ladder he was climbing. He fell, the ladder on top of him, and the second bottle was smashed to pieces. To make matters worse when he came back he smelled terrible and all the crew were seasick.

Eight miles west of Point Lynas I noticed the lifeboat was plunging, sometimes halfway up to the mast. Something was amiss, I had never seen her doing this. I preferred to be on my own at the wheel, I wanted no one to distract my concentration, so I always ordered all the crew under the shelter of the canopy. But that day my vision was impaired by salt water in my eyes—I was, after all, sixty-one years old at that time—so I had my son, David, and Murley, the two youngest and most agile members of the crew, to stand there with me.

Suddenly the *Watkin* leaped out of the water—later the coastguards, who were watching us, told me that often we were clear out of the water—and I could see two gaping holes in the foredeck. I immediately ordered my mechanic, Evan Owen, to reduce speed. We wouldn't normally have used high speeds in such conditions, but the coastguards kept asking, 'Can't you save these men, Moelfre?' and when you hear that you forget all about the possibility of damage. At slower speeds, the boat answered better to the helm and I was able to send Murley and David forward to find out what damage had been done. It was dangerous; they could easily have been swept overboard. But, if I sent anybody, I had to send my own son. If I had sent someone else and they had been washed overboard I'd have to live with the reputation of saving my own son at the expense of my crew. It had to be David. Murley I could not have kept back anyway. I watched with my heart in my mouth while they crawled forward and I don't think I breathed again until they were back.

They told me that the force of the sea had ripped away the two deck ventilators and the bow of the lifeboat was full of water. As a temporary repair they had plugged the holes with spare sou'westers.

I had to drive on at full speed, shouting to the crew to hold on for their lives every time the lifeboat jumped out of the sea. As it happened the extra weight of the water we had shipped worked to our advantage. It kept the *Watkin* lower in the sea. We were rapidly approaching the Skerries rocks, but we still did not know where we were. Were we inside the rocks? We could see hardly anything, only clouds of spray lashed by the wind. My eyes were by now caked with salt. There was no wheel-house shelter in that lifeboat and the man at the wheel took all the sea. But I knew we could not be far from West Mouse Island.

Murley shouted: 'I think I've seen something dead ahead.' The sun came out as it usually does before sunset and there was the *Nafsiporos* about a mile on our starboard bow. I knew I was clear of the rocks and, as we approached the Greek ship, I saw the Holyhead lifeboat hove-to, head on to the sea, waiting to go in to take the crew off.

I knew it was going to be very difficult to get the crew off because the sea was really nasty. There's very strong currents along the Skerries there and the ship was lying broadside to the breaking sea. It was going to be difficult to get alongside.

In such a gale, the Holyhead crew had been surprised to see a helicopter approaching from the land. It was getting darkish at about 4.15, and its lights were blinking. It had been able to get airborne from the RAF station at Valley, only after the crew manhandled the machine into the lee of a hangar where, in the less disturbed air, it could take off. The helicopter made two attempts at hovering. The pilot had to fly at 60mph in order to hover above the ship; at a lower speed he was swept down wind. With the force of wind and the extreme rolling of the freighter, it was impossible for him to lower a man down on his winch wire to effect the rescue.

When the helicopter's attempt failed, it was the Holyhead lifeboat's turn to try. William Jones, then second coxswain, remembers the scene: 'There was no way at all on her. Cox'n Alcock came round her stern and made the first approach. For a moment I thought we'd had it: I thought the *Nafsiporos* was going to roll over us. The sea had lifted her high in the air and her screw was churning round above our heads. I really thought she was going to crash down on us. It was frightening.'

The Greek freighter's crew had turned out the ship's starboard lifeboat in her davits, but with the crazy motion of the ship they had let go the forward rope and the boat was swinging on a single davit. The men on both the Holyhead and Moelfre lifeboats realized the danger this would be to anyone trying to get alongside.

William Jones continues:

> The ship's lifeboat had slid away just as we came round the stern and it was only a few feet away from the jumping ladder. A wave slammed us against the steel plates of the *Nafsiporos* and we had to sheer away. As we circled, all of us were looking for a safe approach but that lifeboat was always in the way. We shouted through the loud-hailer for the crew to cut it away, but either they could not hear or they could not understand our Welsh accents. In any case that lifeboat remained where it was.

The watching lifeboatmen knew that time was running out for the freighter. She had drifted past the Ethel Rock buoy with only yards to spare and, although her crew had managed to get her port anchor down, it failed to hold. When, finally, the anchor did bite, *Nafsiporos* was only ¼ mile west of the East Mouse Rock. She was held in 6 fathoms of water in a 5-knot ebb-tide and yawing 35 degrees either side of the vertical. The sun had set and, with 100mph winds and waves 35ft high, conditions for a lifeboat rescue could not have been worse. The jumping ladder, down which the men would climb when the order was given to abandon ship, was only half a boat's length from the dangling lifeboat.

As a matter of courtesy, the *Watkin*, well inside the *St Cybi*'s patrol area, stood by while the Holyhead boat made the first run. Dick remembers:

> The radio on both lifeboats was out of order because of the severe battering we had taken. It was dark by now and I did not know how many of the crew the Holyhead lifeboat had rescued. I decided to approach. There was a strong ebb-tide running from east to west. We went close in towards the ship which was rolling very, very heavily. By lowering the anchor the crew had hoped to keep the ship's head up to wind, but the tide was too strong and it made going alongside difficult. After calculating the speed

> of the tide and setting against that the speed of the lifeboat, I turned the *Watkin* away, made a circle and approached from the west, edging nearer and nearer to the side.

Twice Dick defied enormous seas and got alongside, but he could not persuade any of the terrified Greek crew to leave their ship and for a while her young captain refused to give the order to abandon.

On the Holyhead boat, a difficult decision faced Cox'n Alcock in his first big rescue. His bowman, who had been ill, was not on board. Alcock was the only man in the boat experienced enough to snatch the crewmen now scrambling down the jump-ladder slung over the freighter's side. It would need split-second timing and the ship's boat would be swinging over his head as he stood in the bows. The obvious man to take his place as coxswain of the *St Cybi* was Lieut-Commander Harvey, who was serving as a crew member. Alcock called him over and, when the lifeboat went in for her first rescue attempt, Harvey was behind the wheel and Alcock stood on the fore-deck with his second cox, William Jones.

Commander Harvey takes up the story:

> We found ourselves—by adjusting our ropes on both engines and positioning ourselves to the tide, using both engines and the rudder—laying down on her, so that when we made contact beam-on we hit the bottom of the jumping ladder. Now we were 15 or 20ft up the ladder and, as we tossed and rolled alongside her, we managed to take off five Greek seamen. The first man was rather loath to leave the ladder and had, literally to be muffled away by our crew on deck.

Suddenly Harvey shouted a desperate warning and put the

engines full astern. The *St Cybi*, riding high on a wave, had struck the ship's boat. Its remaining rope snapped and Alcock and Jones had to jump to safety as she came crashing on to the lifeboat's deck. The short mast, which carries the exhaust, buckled under the impact and the boat's gear spilled out everywhere, her oars crashing through the open windows of the wheel-house. The boat had hit the deck upside-down, bending the guard rail stanchions in every direction. Fortunately, the movement of the *St Cybi*, as she gathered stern way, and a helpful wave which washed over the deck, dislodged the boat and carried her overboard, taking the guard rail with her and leaving debris scattered all over the lifeboat's deck.

Now it was the turn of the Moelfre boat to go alongside, no easy task after the near disaster her crew had just witnessed. But Dick had confidence in his men. Murley Francis, Hugh Owen, Evan Owen and Hugh Jones had all been with him on the *Hindlea* rescue; the courage of second mechanic William Maynard Davies was beyond question and Dick had no fears about his son. The remaining member of his crew, Captain David Jeavons, gave him no cause for concern either. Though it was his first service in the boat, he had been master of six Canadian Pacific Steamship vessels, ranging from 3,500 to 27,500 tons, and his next command was to be the *Empress of England*. The captain's normal trade was in the North Atlantic so he was no stranger to rough weather. All that day he had worked as a deck-hand and Dick wondered how he must be feeling, only 3ft above the sea, when his customary bridge on a liner was so high over the water.

Captain Jeavons recalls:

> The sea and weather on 2 December was certainly not what deep-sea men would regard as boating weather. To call conditions extreme is really an under-estimation and I

> was truly impressed by the strength of the lifeboats. Both of them were unavoidably thrown against the bucking sides of the Greek vessel with tremendous force and impact. That they both survived the ordeal without being totally wrecked I think is a miracle in itself, and the strength and calm of their crews is beyond praise.

As Dick brought the *Watkin* round and ran alongside the *Nafsiporos*, a wave hit her abeam and the lifeboat crashed against the side of the stricken ship.

'Our boat being small it was being tossed about very, very badly,' Dick remembers. 'We managed to get alongside after judging the speed of the tide and counteracting that with the speed of the boat. My biggest worry was to keep her steady by the jumping ladders, so that she wouldn't go forward or backwards, to give them a chance to jump.

'We were like a ball being thrown against the gable end of a house. She bounced back and back again to the side of the ship. I knew we were badly damaged, but there was no time for anything else now except saving the men. And this is where I want to pay a very high tribute to my wonderful crew for the gallant way they stood and literally plucked the crew of the Greek ship off on to our lifeboat. They behaved magnificently.

'All my crew were on deck and, as the lifeboat rose up on a wave, Murley and David grabbed the men on the ladder and passed them along to the others who took them under the canopy. We managed to take off ten in this way, but there were still four men aboard, including the captain. I was shouting my head off, probably in Welsh, for them to come to the lifeboat, and they were shouting back, in Greek, that they were not leaving the ship. In the end they stayed on her and when the weather eased they were towed back to Liverpool.'

Captain Jeavons recalls:

The men on deck on the port side of both those lifeboats took terrible risks. The *Nafsiporos* and the lifeboat were roaring towards each other, which meant there was every chance that the men on the port side would be totally crushed against the side of the Greek ship. As Commander Harvey said, the seamen were reluctant to leave and had to be dragged off the side; this meant that the men on deck were on the port side for a long period of time, taking an extreme personal risk. I myself was amidships, catching the men as they were thrown across and consequently was not in as much danger. I was therefore able to observe the risk being taken by these other men. One other thing: the engineers were absolutely terrific. The remarkable response from the engine room—instructions had to be shouted over the noise of the wind and sea—undoubtedly averted disaster on that day.

Dick continues:

The lifeboat was badly damaged. The electric power had been knocked out, the compass was wrecked. We had no lights and I was in strange water. Fortunately the the Holyhead boat stood off Carmel Head to guide us into Holyhead harbour, 7 miles away. We had to navigate very carefully, as it was pitch dark, but we eventually tied up at Holyhead.

By the time they came ashore the Moelfre crew had not eaten for twenty-three hours. Dick, a man in his sixties, had not had the wheel out of his hands for twelve and a half hours.

The Holyhead lifeboatmen, after landing survivors and seeing four injured Greek seamen taken off by ambulance, put to sea once more to stand by the *Nafsiporos*. Four men were still on board and the vessel was in grave danger of breaking up on the rocks.

The two coxswains had agreed that the Moelfre boat should relieve the Holyhead boat at 6am. Happily the storm abated and the Dutch tug *Utrecht*—which had been assisting the *Vinland*—was free to take the *Nafsiporos* in tow through the rocks to safety.

At a meeting of the Committee of Management of the RNLI on 12 January 1967, Lieut-Commander Harvey and Cox'n Richard Evans were each awarded gold medals for truly outstanding skill and tremendous courage. This was the first time a gold medal had been awarded to a lifeboat inspector for an actual rescue, while Dick was the first man since Cox'n Robert Cox of the Humber lifeboat in January 1943, to win a second gold medal. Silver medals were awarded to Cox'n Thomas Alcock and motor mechanic Eric Jones of the *St Cybi*, and to Evan Owen, of the *Watkin Williams*; in atrocious conditions, almost completely under water, they had remained at the engine controls throughout the rescue. The crews of both lifeboats won bronze medals for their gallantry.

The Moelfre crew gather to wish Dick 'God speed' in his retirement (*RNLI*)

Dick's coldest memories weren't at sea. They were during this fund raising drive in the London to Brighton vintage car race (*Daily Express*)

8

NO RETIREMENT

When Dick went to London on lifeboat business he was always delighted if Dan Kirkpatrick, coxswain of the Longhope lifeboat, from Hoy Island in the Orkneys, was among the RNLI party at the Berners Hotel. Dan, a tall, shy man of the Orkneys, had been coxswain of the Longhope lifeboat—the 47ft *TGB*—since 1955. For his services at sea, he had received three silver medals and a number of citations. Two of his silver medals had been awarded for rescues of Aberdeen trawlers: the *Strathcoe* in February 1959 and the *Ben Barjas* in 1964. He won a third clasp to his silver in April 1965 for saving fifteen men from the trawler *Ross Puma*. *Reed's Nautical Almanac* described his patrol area in the Pentland Firth—the strip of the North Sea which separates the Orkneys from the Scottish mainland—as 'the most difficult navigational passage of the coasts of the United Kingdom'.

The two coxswains had become close friends and, when they met in the hotel, they would stay up talking lifeboats, long after their wives had gone to bed. Dan was not a fanciful man and something he once said in the early hours had shocked Dick. It had come, an outburst almost, landing in their conversation like a fish in the bottom of a boat.

'Y'know, we're mad, the two of us,' Dan Kirkpatrick said. 'There's only one way all this taking of risks can end and we both know it.'

Dick could admit to his own fears. True bravery is the degree to which we overcome fear, but he had never thought of disaster and death as inevitable. He remembered uneasily the Orcadian reputation for second sight and as soon as he could he made an excuse and went to bed.

He often thought of Dan's remark in the months that followed. Then, on 16 March 1969, he opened his paper and read: EIGHT HEROES DIE AS LIFEBOAT CAPSIZES IN STORM.

Dan Kirkpatrick had died on the day he was to have gone to London to receive his third silver medal.

Dick tried to imagine how the disaster had come about. A telephone call from the lifeboat secretary would send Dan and his son, Roy, hurrying along the narrow cliff path to the red corrugated-iron boat-house. He pictured the crew arriving, one by one, within seconds of the maroon exploding. Dick knew them all by reputation. Dan had talked of them lovingly, like a father—as, indeed, to two of them he was.

The Longhope lifeboat crew was drawn from two families. Dan's close friend, Bob 'Sodjer' Johnstone, an ex-army man, would have arrived at the boat-house with his two sons, Robbie, who lived next door to his father, and Jimmy, who lived only fifty yards from the boat-house. Jock Kirkpatrick, Dan's second son, would almost certainly be the last to arrive. He was not on the phone and lived three miles from the station.

Dick looked at the last name mentioned in the newspaper story, E. McFadyen. That would be 'Wee Ericky' who had hung around the lifeboat station since he could walk. He was in sea school at Kirkwall, studying for a mate's ticket. He must have been on leave, Dick thought, and nobody could have prevented him from joining the crew as an extra man.

They would all climb aboard the *TGB* and plunge helter-skelter down the slipway into the sea. In the cottage on the cliff Dan's wife, Margaret, would build up the fire, turn the radio dial to the trawler wavelength, and settle down to wait and pray for her menfolk.

According to the newspaper account, the Longhope crew had been called out to the aid of a 2,600-ton Liberian vessel, *Irene*, on passage in ballast from Leith to Norway. Like the *Nafsiporos*, she was drifting, out of control and at the mercy of the wind. Her position had been reported half an hour before the *TGB* was launched. She was only 3 miles from the rocks off the west coast of South Ronaldsay, in the Orkneys.

Another lifeboat, the 70ft *Grace Paterson Ritchie*, the second biggest in the RNLI, was launched from Kirkwall ten minutes later to join the search. She cast off from the harbour wall and headed north for the open sea. Help was on its way to *Irene* from two directions—the *Grace Paterson Ritchie* from the north and the *TGB* from the south. Dick could picture Dan lashed to the wheel, straining for a glimpse of rocks or shipping, as he put the *TGB* through the Pentland tide-race round the southern tip of South Ronaldsay. It was a nasty stretch of water. Dan and 'Sodjer', the second cox, would be facing each other across the after-cabin, bracing themselves against the bulkheads.

The *TGB* was spotted by the South Ronaldsay lookout a mile east of the Isle of Swona and 3 miles from *Irene*. He reported: 'She was coming down fast in the flood-tide. Three or four times her mast light disappeared completely. I've rarely seen the race like it was that night.'

Irene meanwhile had grounded off Grim Ness, a spit of cliff on the north-east of the island. She had made a 'Not Under Control' signal and sent up flares. Her position was radioed to the lifeboats.

From the *TGB*, 'Sodjer' radioed back: 'This is the Longhope lifeboat on course and proceeding towards the *Irene*.'

It was the last message from the *TGB*.

At 9.30pm the lookout took his eyes away for a moment from the window where he had been watching the lights of the lifeboat as she tossed through the race. When he looked back the lights had gone.

Alex McDonald, principal keeper of the Skerries light in the middle of the race, saw her at the same time. 'The weather was terrible,' he later told reporters.

John Rich and Eric Malcolm, his assistant keepers, had been on a rock 50ft below. 'We saw her just off the north-east of the light,' Eric said. 'Her mast lights were going down into the water and disappearing for seconds at a time. We decided to go into the radio hut to hear what was going on. When we looked out again there was no sign of the Longhope boat.'

Shortly after 9.30pm *Irene* grounded in a position which made lifeboat rescue impossible. At 10.05pm Wick radio put out the message to recall both lifeboats. Only the *Grace Paterson Ritchie* answered.

Irene's crew of seventeen Algerians and Greeks were already safe. They had been swung ashore by breeches buoy by the time—11.15pm—the *Grace Paterson Ritchie*, fighting mountainous seas all the way, reached South Ronaldsay. There was no sign of the Longhope boat.

A member of the Kirkwall crew, Jimmie Craigie, recalled:

> You could feel the grief like a blanket over the boat. Nobody spoke, but you could almost hear their thoughts. I kept hoping inside it was a radio failure. There had been radio silences on boats before and they had turned up all right. I thought of my mother listening to the radio at home, worrying about her worrying about me. But we knew. The Longhope boys had gone.

Dick knew too. In his brick house in Moelfre, he sat, with the newspaper on his knees, writing in his mind the rest of the tragic story. He imagined Margaret Kirkpatrick sitting by a dying fire, a waking dawn breaking beyond the windows of the cottage, knowing by the things that were not being said on the radio that something had gone terribly wrong. He thought of the wives who had lost their husbands and a widow her son. The men in the *Grace Paterson Ritchie* would have waited impatiently on the edge of the race for darkness to lift. While Dick was reading about the rescue, they would be in the heart of the race, searching. Other boats would join them, and aircraft too—Shackletons, most likely, and helicopters.

In the event the *TGB* made her own macabre way back. On the following Tuesday evening she was sighted only a few miles from her home station on Hoy Island. She had returned, upside-down, on the tide. There were seven bodies still inside her, but James Swanson was never found.

At an official inquiry into the disaster, held in Kirkwall, it was decided that the *TGB* had capsized in maelstrom conditions. The crew of the *Grace Paterson Ritchie*, giving evidence, described the wave they believed had caused the loss of the lifeboat. One of them, Dan Grieve, said:

> It was black dark and our boat just started to rise and rise. It was a mountain. Billy Sinclair and me dropped down to our knees to see if we could squint up and see the white top of it. We couldn't. We could just see that great lump of water. I shouted to Iain Thompson at the wheel to get down. I thought that when she broke through the water would bring the glass in.
>
> She went down that wave on her nose. Don't ask me how big it was, but Billy Sinclair counted seven seconds before she bottomed out in the trough. He says it was 100ft from crest to trough. He's a master mariner. He knows. I know I'd go through hell in that boat after that. But I don't believe a smaller boat like the *TGB* could have survived.
>
> That rogue wave hit us just about the time she disappeared. It hit her and got her.

When, later, Dick read these words he remembered what Dan Kirkpatrick had said that night in the Berners Hotel.

Ten months after that tragedy, another lifeboat, the *Duchess of Kent*, capsized off Kinnaird Head on the Aberdeenshire coast. Launched from Fraserburgh, she had gone to the aid of the Danish vessel *Opel* which had sprung a leak in a 50mph gale. As the *Duchess of Kent* was escorting the *Opel* she was overturned by gigantic seas. Miraculously, mechanic John Buchan was thrown clear and dragged aboard the Russian trawler, *Logger*, which had answered the *Opel*'s SOS. Another Russian vessel, *Viktor Kingslepp*, succeeded in righting the lifeboat and lashed it to the ship's side. Four bodies were still inside. Helicopters and Shackletons searched until darkness fell, but the fifth man was not found.

The cruiser HMS *Londonderry* took the lifeboat back to her home station where a group of silent watchers waited. The dead crew members, all from Fraserburgh, were assistant harbourmaster John Stephen, father of two; Fred Kirkness, married with a son; William Hadden, father of four; John Buchan and Joseph Buchan.

Mrs Stella Jackson Buchan was one wife for whom the ordeal of waiting for news had a happy outcome. For three hours she knew that only one out of three unrelated Buchans in the crew had been saved. Not until she heard her husband's voice over the radio, translating for the Russian ship which saved his life, did she find out he was safe.

The Fraserburgh and the Longhope boats that capsized were both Watson class, like the *Watkin Williams*. As Dick read the reports of the Board of Trade inquiry into the loss of the Fraserburgh lifeboat, he could not help wondering how long his luck would hold. The *Duchess of Kent* had been adversely affected by minor modifications and re-engining in 1965. He read on:

> . . . other Watson-class lifeboats with similar transverse stability characteristics could not be guaranteed to survive in the sort of weather which it would meet off the north and north-west coast of Scotland . . . There was no criticism of the boat as such but rather a suggestion that there might be a limitation of the conditions in which she could operate . . .

Conditions like those Dick had faced in the *Hindlea* service and again when he went out in the *Watkin Williams* to the *Nafsiporos* must fall far beyond such a 'limitation'. Not for the first time he realized how close he and his crew had come to sharing the fate of the men in the Longhope and Fraserburgh boats.

Under the rules of the RNLI, Dick was due to retire when he reached the age of sixty-five on 19 January 1970. Secretly, he was not sorry. The death of Dan Kirkpatrick and his crew and the tragedy of the Fraserburgh boat had affected him deeply. He had felt enormous sympathy for Dan's widow, Margaret, and remembered a remark she made after the tragedy: 'Every time he put out I had the feeling that something was going to happen. For years it never had and they always came home safely. But that feeling was always there.' He wondered whether the same thoughts had run through Nansi's mind whenever she watched him leave the house on a service.

'Dan and I both had three sons who were members of our respective crews and wives who suffered mental anguish when our sons went out with us in the lifeboat. We had both been involved in major rescues. You can imagine my feelings when we first knew that this brave man and two of his sons had been lost on rescue. And then, only ten months later, we were mourning another crew, another lifeboat lost. I thought how fortunate I had been to have come through my seventeen years as cox'n unharmed. Yet, despite all, I dreaded the day when I would have to retire and hand the lifeboat over to another cox'n. I always regarded her as *my* lifeboat. I knew Murley was a competent cox and had the qualities to make a success of the job.

'I had no worries about handing over, but I was very uneasy about my own future,' Dick went on. 'Then I received a letter from the RNLI saying they would like to see me in London. I couldn't understand what this was all about because I had no intention of staying in the service and the whole family was behind me. Before I went to London all my sons came round and said that whatever the RNLI offered I must refuse to stay on. My boys said that it would be unfair on me, on my crew and, above all, on Nansi.

'The people at head office couldn't have been nicer. "Well, Cox'n Evans," they said, "the time has come for us to part, but we don't want to lose you."

'I said, "Well, I don't want to be sixty-five either."

"But we'd like to keep you on."

"Thank you very much, gentlemen," I said, "but I think it's time for me to go now."

"We don't want you to go in the lifeboat again. We want you to go round the country lecturing for us."

'I was absolutely stunned. Me, a tough, hard lifeboat cox'n, going round lecturing? It was impossible. "D'you mean going on a platform in front of an audience and speaking to them?"

' "We know you can do it."

'I was getting a bit fed up with all this. "Surely I know my own capabilities better than you?"

' "Would you listen to this tape recorder?"

'Somebody was speaking about the Institution. I thought, "Boy, that's quite good, that English." They stopped the tape and asked me, "What do you think of that?"

'I said, "Listen here, gentlemen. I'm a Welsh-speaking Welshman. I speak nothing but Welsh with my family and my friends. You don't expect me to speak English like that, do you?"

'But it *was* me! They had recorded me thanking the Institution at a big dinner in London. I couldn't believe I could speak English like that. I still quibbled about taking it on—I'd much rather go out in a lifeboat on a stormy night—but I agreed to have a try.

'The first place I was sent to was Manchester. They might as well have sent me to the middle of Anglesey because so many people came to the island from Manchester on their holidays. Manchester Town Hall was packed. But I still dreaded going on the platform. Indeed when I stood up I was shaking like a leaf and when I raised a foot it sounded like tap-dancing. I'd been writing a speech out for several weeks and I'd memorized every full stop and comma in it. I kept studying it in the train all the way to Manchester. The funny thing is that although I spoke on that platform for twenty-five minutes I never spoke a single word that was in the speech.'

Soon after that Dick went to London to speak at the Guildhall. 'This worried me a great deal. I'd read about it in the papers and in books but, goodness me, the thought of speaking there . . .'

The evening went well, and other speaking dates followed every two weeks. Gradually Dick found he was enjoying his new role.

'I was very concerned about my ungrammatical English. You must understand I went to sea when I was fourteen years of age and my education is limited. Before I started my talk I used to say: "I don't profess to be a public speaker. I'm sure you have all understood by now that I am a Welsh-speaking Welshman and that I am very proud of it. Whatever I attempt to say to you here is thought out in Welsh and then automatically translated into English. So I'm giving you two speeches in one. If you don't understand my English I will explain it to you—in Welsh.'

Dick's Welsh accent was in fact a great success. On his second Guildhall visit to speak at the RNLI's 150th anniversary dinner, he was given a standing ovation, an honour previously accorded only to Sir Alec Douglas Home and Sir Harold Macmillan. So proficient has he become that in 1977 he won the RNLI Public Relations Award.

The list of Dick's honours and awards is an impressive one:

1940 Thanks on vellum, RNLI
1943 Bronze Medal, RNLI
1959 Gold medal, RNLI
1960 HM the Queen's silver medal for gallantry at sea
1967 Gold medal, RNLI
1967 'Man of the Year' award
1969 British Empire Medal
1975 Honorary Fellow, Manchester Polytechnic
1978 Honorary Bard, National Eisteddfod

From the time Dick joined the crew in 1921 until his retirement almost half a century later, the Moelfre lifeboat made 179 launches and saved 281 lives. The men of the station have been awarded more decorations than any other in Britain: four RNLI gold medals (the 'Lifeboat VC'), twenty-six silver and twenty-nine bronze, including five HM the Queen's Silver Medals, fifteen Royal Humane Society medals and one British Empire Medal.

Dick, who is the only living lifeboatman to have received two gold medals, has become a celebrity. He has met every member of the royal family except, ironically, the sailor Duke of Edinburgh. He has been to three royal garden parties, and he and Nansi have been guests at one of the

Queen's private cocktail parties at Buckingham Palace. The late Princess Marina, Duchess of Kent, was patron of the RNLI and one of Dick's admirers. On 27 May 1960, during a visit to Wales, she made a point of visiting Anglesey so that Dick and his crew could take her for a trip round Moelfre Bay in the *Watkin Williams*. In 1967, the year after the *Nafsiporos* episode, Dick was among those nominated by the RNLI for a 'Man of the Year' award. With Jack Hawkins, the actor who had gallantly overcome the loss of his voice through cancer, and other brave men of that year, he attended the presentation ceremony. Visitors to Moelfre began to include Dick in their holiday snapshots. His face grins out of the pages of family albums all over the country.

'I have been lucky,' Dick told reporters, after he had retired. 'I have had a loyal and trustworthy crew who trusted me with their lives. There's a new young crew now, and a young cox'n. I haven't any doubt they'll attempt to do all the things we did in the past.'

Poor gallant Murley Francis, who took over command of the boat from Dick, was to die ironically in his bed after a short illness a year later; he was only forty-one.

The second coxswain was to be veteran Hugh Owen, a lifeboatman for forty-three years and the only surviving member of the crew which went on service to the *Excel*. He has been awarded three RNLI bronze medals, the Queen's silver medal and the Shipwreck Society's silver medal.

Moelfre lifeboat station was crowded for Dick's farewell party. Two hundred well-wishers sang 'For he's a jolly good fellow'; there were three hundred telegrams, including one from the master and crew of *Nafsiporos*, and another from Cledwyn Hughes, Anglesey's MP and at that time Minister of Agriculture; the crew of the Beaumaris lifeboat, which was on exercise in the bay, came inshore to pay their respects. The traditional retirement launch unfortunately had to be cancelled. A south-easterly gale, Dick's old adversary, would have prevented the lifeboat getting back on the slipway.

Dick made a speech from the stern of the boat. The new honorary secretary of the RNLI branch, Thomas Owen, and the minister, the Reverend T. A. Smith, both spoke a few words, and then it was all over.

'I went out silently and went home,' Dick recalls. 'I was pretty dejected. My world had tumbled down. I was supposed to be on duty until midnight, but I phoned Murley.

' "Murley, it's all yours now," I told him. "Don't call me if you get a call before midnight. If there's a service say that I am not very well and you take it."

'He laughed. "Oh, no," he said. "You're on duty till midnight and I'm not taking over till then. I'm taking my wife out."

'The weeks that followed were like a new world. I had been used to going down to the boat-house every morning and I missed the company of my crew very much. There was no use fretting, old age creeps on us all and we can do nothing about it. I well remember being in chapel one Sunday morning when the maroons calling the lifeboat were fired. I instinctively dropped my hymn book and I had reached the door of the chapel before I realized I was no longer wanted. Believe me, it was a terrible feeling.'

Among the guests at the farewell ceremony were two smartly dressed girls whom Dick did not know. When he saw them asking questions of his crew, he assumed they were journalists. A few days later he caught sight of them again. 'There are two smart young girls in a car outside Mr Price's next door,' Dick told Nansi, and he wondered why she looked so startled.

It was the first of a series of odd things which began to happen.

David arrived one day and started asking his father funny questions he had never asked before.

'Who was your best pal at school, Dad? . . . What did you used to do when you were a little boy, what were you playing? How old were you when you learned to swim?'

'My God,' said Dick, 'you've waited a long time before asking me these things.'

Every time the phone rang, Nansi rushed to answer it. Dick began to get suspicious. One day he answered it himself and heard a girl's voice ask 'Is that 529?'

'Yes,' said Dick.

'Sorry,' the voice replied. 'Wrong number.'

'How daft can people be?' he asked Nansi. 'Why did she ask "is that 529?" then say, "Wrong number"?'

Six weeks later Dick was called to London to speak at a special function. Unusually, on this occasion Nansi was not invited. As she packed his case, Dick was surprised to see she was putting in his best suit.

'I've just bought that,' he protested. 'Expensive too. My green suit I travel in is quite good enough. I can't be struggling up and down the underground with a heavy case.'

Downstairs another surprise awaited him. William had arrived to give him a lift to the station.

'I've got a car of my own,' said Dick, testy by now, but his son insisted.

'Please take the dark suit,' Nansi called from the bedroom and Dick did something he had never done in his married life—he swore at her. As soon as the words left his lips he regretted it.

He was silent as they drove to Bangor. 'Be sure to tell your mother I'm very sorry,' he said, as he got on the train. He was wondering why William was in such a hurry to see him off—and who was the man on the platform looking at him so suspiciously and then moving quickly away? It made him uneasy.

In London a car was waiting and a chauffeur he had never seen before took him to the Rubens Hotel. Dick always telephoned his wife to tell her that he had arrived safely. After the incident that morning he was more than anxious to talk to her, but when he rang there was no reply. Dick hardly slept a wink that night, fearing Nansi was hurt by what he had said. The next morning he telephoned again, but there was still no reply. Between his speaking engagements, he tried several more times to reach her but without success. Thoroughly upset by now, he went to RNLI headquarters where he was surprised to be told 'the boss' Admiral Sir Wilfred Woods, wanted to see him.

'Now,' said the admiral, 'we've decided you are going to have lunch with your old friend Commander Harvey.' This too was unusual and Dick began to wonder why he was getting such VIP treatment.

Totally bemused, Dick found himself in a taxi which looked nothing like a taxi, being taken by a driver in dark glasses miles out of London to luncheon. After making another speech, Dick had just had time to call in at head office before catching the 5.30 train home. The admiral wanted to see him again.

'I'm in a tearing hurry,' Dick explained.

'I'm very sorry, Dick,' said the admiral. 'You won't be going by that train today. Something has cropped up and you have to face a very large audience.'

'Good God,' said Dick, 'I've done four speeches already. I'll do it, but I've got to notify my wife.'

'I'll ring for you,' said the admiral, but once again there was no reply.

Dick felt sure something was desperately wrong. 'I've tried seven times,' he told him, much upset.

'Come, come,' said Sir Wilfred. 'If there was anything wrong, the first place to be notified would be this office. Your telephone's out of order, depend on it. It's not ringing out.'

Commander Harvey insisted on coming with Dick to the

meeting. He seemed unusually anxious. 'You've got to be there on the dot of 7pm.'

'Good God, no,' said Dick. 'They'll be reading the minutes of the previous meeting.'

'That is an order,' said the Commander, suddenly brusque. 'And go to the toilet.'

'I don't want to go to the toilet.'

'You'll be there for three hours.'

'I don't care, I don't want to.'

'Well, for God's sake, come with me then, I do.'

Dick wondered why Harvey was so nervous.

It was a very smart cloakroom. Two young ladies appeared and began brushing his clothes.

Dead on 7pm Dick walked through a door and on to a stage. He was shown to a seat and waited for the man to introduce him to an audience he could barely see for the glare of a bank of footlights. The man's face seemed familiar.

'Dick Evans,' said the man—and in a flash Dick remembered who he was.

'Good God,' he said, 'you're Eamonn Andrews, aren't you?'

Andrews grinned and smoothly finished his sentence, '. . . This is Your Life.'

ACKNOWLEDGEMENTS
My thanks are due, for their help in collecting photographs, to Ray Kipling, Assistant Press Officer of the RNLI; to Mike Unger, Assistant Editor, *Liverpool Daily Post* and to the *Northern Picture Editors*; Pete Pitilla, *Daily Mail*, John Knill, *Daily Express*, and Bill Mealey, *Daily Mirror*—old friends of many a frolic. To Lynn May for help with the research, to my bossy wife for editing the MSS so painstakingly. And to Jimmie Bell, Viv Bellis and Alan Lund for the use of their accommodation.